Theory Test
Questions
for car drivers
& motorcyclists

2002/2003

Theory Test Questions

for car drivers
& motorcyclists

2002/2003

Including questions and answers valid for
tests taken after 17th September 2001.

Published by BSM
in association with
Virgin Publishing

First published in the UK in 2001 by
The British School of Motoring Ltd
1 Forest Road
Feltham
Middlesex
TW13 7RR

First reprint 2002

ISBN 0 7535 0626 2

Cover picture and cartoons by Marc Lacey

Design, typesetting and reprographics by Thalamus Publishing

Printed in Italy

Contents

Foreword

Driving and riding are enjoyable and valuable life skills which is why every year about a million new learners take to the road, each one of them with one clear aim. This aim is almost certainly the same as yours – to gain their full licence.

There is no substitute for practical experience when learning to drive or ride. The best way to gain this is by taking lessons with a good professional instructor who uses the most up-to-date teaching techniques in a modern, dual-controlled car or on a radio-equipped motorcycle. However, it has always been

equally important to prepare for your driving or riding lessons and, since the introduction of the Theory Test, this is doubly true.

Theory Test Questions contains the revised set (valid for tests after 17th September 2001) of official Driving Standards Agency questions which are currently published and which may be included in the actual examination.

This book is an ideal study aid which allows you to test and revise your knowledge. It has been designed for use in conjunction with its companion volumes, *Pass Your Driving Theory Test, Pass Your Driving Test* and *Practice Sessions*.

Theory Test Questions allows you to check your level of knowledge by presenting you with real examination questions. The questions are set out under topic headings, and as you work through each section you will prove to yourself that you not only understand what you have learnt, but can demonstrate this by answering the question correctly.

In doing so, you will gradually boost your confidence and thereby recognise when you are ready to take and pass your Theory Test.

Your instructor will help you to plan your studies and ensure that you fully understand why the knowledge you acquire is essential to keep you safe on the road, as well as to take you past that first all important hurdle of passing your Theory Test.

There are no short cuts to becoming a safe and competent motorist or motorcyclist, but that does not mean that you cannot enjoy yourself while learning.

Theory Test Questions and its companion volumes will, I hope, bring the Theory Test alive and make it relevant, and at the same time it should also help you develop your driving and riding skills.

In 90 years of teaching people to drive, BSM instructors have helped millions of people pass their driving test. In my view, *Theory Test Questions* completes the best set of books available to help you make the most of your lessons and ensure that you prepare for both the theory and practical parts of your driving or riding test in a structured and positive way.

Keith Cameron
Road Safety Adviser

Keith Cameron is one of Britain's leading authorities on motoring and driver education. He has held a number of senior positions within the Department of Transport, including Chief Driving Examiner where he had responsibility for all UK driving tests.

How to use this book

While it is possible just to see the Theory Test as something you have to do on the way to getting your full car or motorcycle licence, knowing more about safety issues or anything that increases your hazard awareness has got to make you a better and safer driver or rider. However, learning answers to questions without understanding the meaning is not going to improve your skills and probably will not help you greatly in passing your Theory Test. You need to think clearly about what the question is asking and then make sure that you understand how an answer can assist your practical skills.

At the side of each question you will see a picture symbol denoting

a car,

a motorcycle

or both.

These symbols indicate whether the question will appear in the Driving Theory Test, the Motorcycle Theory Test or both. You only need to study the questions applicable to the test that you intend to sit although of course the more you know about other road users the better.

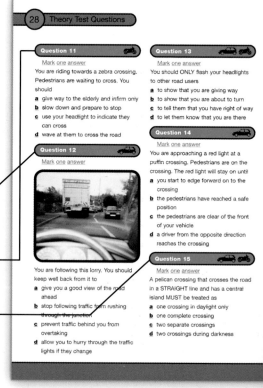

Question 11

Mark one answer

You are riding towards a zebra crossing. Pedestrians are waiting to cross. You should

a give way to the elderly and infirm only
b slow down and prepare to stop
c use your headlight to indicate they can cross
d wave at them to cross the road

Question 12

Mark one answer

You are following this lorry. You should keep well back from it to

a give you a good view of the road ahead
b stop following traffic from rushing through the junction
c prevent traffic behind you from overtaking
d allow you to hurry through the traffic lights if they change

Question 13

Mark one answer

You should ONLY flash your headlights to other road users

a to show that you are giving way
b to show that you are about to turn
c to tell them that you have right of way
d to let them know that you are there

Question 14

Mark one answer

You are approaching a red light at a puffin crossing. Pedestrians are on the crossing. The red light will stay on until

a you start to edge forward on to the crossing
b the pedestrians have reached a safe position
c the pedestrians are clear of the front of your vehicle
d a driver from the opposite direction reaches the crossing

Question 15

Mark one answer

A pelican crossing that crosses the road in a STRAIGHT line and has a central island MUST be treated as

a one crossing in daylight only
b one complete crossing
c two separate crossings
d two crossings during darkness

You can if you like ignore the picture symbols; it may take a little longer to get through the book, but you will benefit from the Theory being reinforced by duplicate questions. Whether you are

approaching traffic lights in a car or on a motorcycle doesn't change the sequence in which the lights appear. And after reading all the questions, when a motorcyclist turns their head to the side, whether you drive a car or ride a motorcycle you will be warned that the rider is probably about to change direction.

Remember when you actually sit the Theory Test that you have time to read the questions thoroughly. Make sure you understand what is being asked. Don't rush or panic, but instead think carefully about each of the suggested answers. Invariably, if you have put the time and effort into studying as suggested above the correct answer or answers will be more than apparent. If you have any queries or areas that you do not understand then please ask your instructor who will be more than happy to assist you.

People will wish you Good Luck before your Theory Test, but you know now that you don't need it!

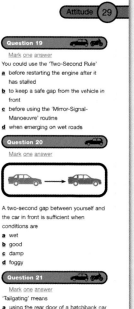

Attitude 29

Question 16

Mark one answer

You are approaching a pelican crossing. The amber light is flashing. You must

a give way to pedestrians who are crossing

b encourage pedestrians to cross

c not move until the green light appears

d stop even if the crossing is clear

Question 17

Mark one answer

You are riding a motorcycle and following a large vehicle at 40mph. You should position yourself

a close behind to make it easier to overtake the vehicle

b to the left of the road to make it easier to be seen

c close behind the vehicle to keep out of the wind

d well back so that you can see past the vehicle

Question 18

Mark one answer

At puffin crossings which light will not show to a driver?

a Flashing amber

b Red

c Steady amber

d Green

Question 19

Mark one answer

You could use the 'Two-Second Rule'

a before restarting the engine after it has stalled

b to keep a safe gap from the vehicle in front

c before using the 'Mirror-Signal-Manoeuvre' routine

d when emerging on wet roads

Question 20

Mark one answer

A two-second gap between yourself and the car in front is sufficient when conditions are

a wet

b good

c damp

d foggy

Question 21

Mark one answer

'Tailgating' means

a using the rear door of a hatchback car

b reversing into a parking space

c following another vehicle too closely

d driving with rear fog lights on

Introduction

The driving test was first introduced to the UK back in 1935. Since that time millions of people have passed the driving test and gained their motoring freedom, many taught by BSM instructors.

In 1996 a separate theory test was introduced for car drivers and provisional motorcyclists, to test their driving and riding knowledge and attitude. This theory test must be passed before a learner can apply for a practical driving or riding test. In January 2000 the theory test was computerised. During your test, questions will appear on a computer screen. You select your answers by simply touching the screen. This 'touch screen' system has been carefully designed to make it easy to use.

BSM centres all have touch screen PCs to test your theory knowledge and allow you to practise using the same technology as you'll find in the actual theory exam. Called Theory Online, access to the BSM computers is available free to anyone taking driving or riding lessons with BSM instructors. For details of your nearest BSM centre please call 08457 276 276.

Theory Test Questions contains the official Driving Standards Agency questions which are currently published and which may be included in the actual examination. That means there are a lot of questions in this book (over 1,000), but when you take your Theory Test, you won't be expected to answer all of them! The Test will only have 35 questions for you to answer.

I am sure your main aim is to pass the Theory Test. Nevertheless, I strongly urge you to do more than simply attempt to learn the answers parrot fashion. Not only will you find such a method of learning very tedious, you will also miss out on the chance to understand the significance of the information you are learning and make use of it when you practise with your instructor.

Plus don't forget to use the BSM Theory online computers to give you the best chance of passing first time.

Theory Test Questions

2001/2002

Alertness

BSM
We won't fail you

Question 1

Mark one answer

You are travelling along this narrow country road. When passing the cyclist you should go

a slowly, sounding the horn as you pass

b quickly, leaving plenty of room

c slowly, leaving plenty of room

d quickly, sounding the horn as you pass

Question 2

Mark one answer

You should always check the 'blind areas' before

a moving off

b slowing down

c changing gear

d giving a signal

Question 3

Mark one answer

Your vehicle is fitted with a hand-held telephone. To use the telephone you should

a reduce your speed

b find a safe place to stop

c steer the vehicle with one hand

d be particularly careful at junctions

Question 4

Mark one answer

The 'blind area' should be checked before

a giving a signal

b applying the brakes

c changing direction

d giving an arm signal

Question 5

Mark one answer

To answer a call on your mobile phone while travelling you should

a reduce your speed wherever you are

b stop in a proper and convenient place

c keep the call time to a minimum

d slow down and allow others to overtake

Question 6

Mark one answer

It is vital to check the 'blind area' before

a changing gear

b giving signals

c slowing down

d changing lanes

Question 7

Mark one answer

Your mobile phone rings while you are on the motorway. Before answering you should

a reduce your speed to 50 mph

b pull up on the hard shoulder

c move into the left-hand lane

d stop in a safe place

Question 8

Mark one answer

Before you make a U-turn in the road, you should

a give an arm signal as well as using your indicators

b signal so that other drivers can slow down for you

c look over your shoulder for a final check

d select a higher gear than normal

Question 9

Mark one answer

To move off safely from a parked position you should

a signal if other drivers will need to slow down

b leave your motorcycle on its stand until the road is clear

c give an arm signal as well as using your indicators

d look over your shoulder for a final check

Question 10

Mark one answer

As a driver what does the term 'Blind Spot' mean?

a An area covered by your right-hand mirror

b An area not covered by your headlights

c An area covered by your left-hand mirror

d An area not seen in your mirrors

Question 11

Mark one answer

When riding, your shoulders obstruct the view in your mirrors. To overcome this you should

a indicate earlier than normal

b fit smaller mirrors

c extend the mirror arms

d brake earlier than normal

Question 12

Mark two answers

Objects hanging from your interior mirror may

a restrict your view

b improve your driving

c distract your attention

d help your concentration

Question 13

Mark two answers

You want to change lanes in busy, moving traffic. Why could looking over your shoulder help?

a Mirrors may not cover blind spots

b To avoid having to give a signal

c So traffic ahead will make room for you

d So your balance will not be affected

e Following motorists would be warned

Question 14

Mark two answers

You are most likely to lose concentration when driving if you

a use a mobile phone

b listen to very loud music

c switch on the heated rear window

d look at the door mirrors

Question 15

Mark one answer

You are about to turn right. What should you do just before you turn?

a Give the correct signal

b Take a 'lifesaver' glance over your shoulder

c Select the correct gear

d Get in position ready for the turn

Question 16

Mark four answers

Which FOUR are most likely to cause you to lose concentration while you are driving?

a Using a mobile phone

b Talking into a microphone

c Tuning your car radio

d Looking at a map

e Checking the mirrors

f Using the demisters

Question 17

Mark one answer

What is the 'lifesaver' when riding a motorcycle?

a A certificate every motorcyclist must have

b A final, rearward glance before changing direction

c A part of the motorcycle tool kit

d A mirror fitted to check blind spots

Question 18

Mark one answer

You are driving on a wet road. You have to stop your vehicle in an emergency. You should

a apply the handbrake and footbrake together

b keep both hands on the wheel

c select reverse gear

d give an arm signal

Question 19

Mark one answer

You see road signs showing a sharp bend ahead. What should you do?

a Continue at the same speed

b Slow down as you go around the bend

c Slow down as you come out of the bend

d Slow down before the bend

Question 20

Mark three answers

As you approach this bridge you should

a move into the middle of the road to get a better view

b slow down

c get over the bridge as quickly as possible

d consider using your horn

e find another route

f beware of pedestrians

Question 21

Mark one answer

When following a large vehicle you should keep well back because

a it allows you to corner more quickly

b it helps the large vehicle to stop more easily

c it allows the driver to see you in the mirrors

d it helps you to keep out of the wind

Question 22

Mark one answer

In which of these situations should you avoid overtaking?

a Just after a bend

b In a one-way street

c On a 30mph road

d Approaching a dip in the road

Question 23

Mark four answers

Which of the following may cause loss of concentration on a long journey?

a Loud music

b Arguing with a passenger

c Using a mobile phone

d Putting in a cassette tape

e Stopping regularly to rest

f Pulling up to tune the radio

Question 24

Mark one answer

You should not use a mobile phone whilst driving

a until you are satisfied that no other traffic is near

b unless you are able to drive one-handed

c because it might distract your attention from the road ahead

d because reception is poor when the engine is running

Question 25

Mark one answer

Your vehicle is fitted with a hands-free phone system. Using this equipment while driving

a is quite safe as long as you slow down

b could distract your attention from the road

c is recommended by The Highway Code

d could be very good for road safety

Question 26

Mark one answer

You are riding at night. You have your headlight on main beam. Another vehicle is overtaking you. When should you dip your headlight?

a When the other vehicle signals to overtake

b As soon as the other vehicle moves out to overtake

c As soon as the other vehicle passes you

d After the other vehicle pulls in front of you

Question 27

Mark one answer

Using a hands-free phone is likely to

a improve your safety

b increase your concentration

c reduce your view

d divert your attention

Question 28

Mark one answer

On a motorcycle you should only use a mobile telephone when you

a have a pillion passenger to help

b have parked in a safe place

c have a motorcycle with automatic gears

d are travelling on a quiet road

Question 29

Mark one answer

Using a mobile phone while you are driving

a is acceptable in a vehicle with power steering

b will reduce your field of vision

c could distract your attention from the road

d will affect your vehicle's electronic systems

Question 30

Mark one answer

You are riding at night and are dazzled by the headlights of an oncoming car. You should

a slow down or stop

b close your eyes

c flash your headlight

d turn your head away

Question 31

Mark one answer

This road marking warns

a drivers to use the hard shoulder

b overtaking drivers there is a bend to the left

c overtaking drivers to move back to the left

d drivers that it is safe to overtake

Question 32

Mark one answer

Your mobile phone rings while you are travelling. You should

a stop immediately

b answer it immediately

c pull up in a suitable place

d pull up at the nearest kerb

Question 33

Mark one answer

You are riding along a motorway. You see an accident on the other side of the road. Your lane is clear. You should

a assist the emergency services

b stop, and cross the road to help

c concentrate on what is happening ahead

d place a warning triangle in the road

Question 34

Mark one answer

You should ONLY use a mobile phone when

a receiving a call
b suitably parked
c driving at less than 30 mph
d driving an automatic vehicle

Question 35

Mark one answer

What is the safest way to use a mobile phone in your vehicle?

a Use hands-free equipment
b Find a suitable place to stop
c Drive slowly on a quiet road
d Direct your call through the operator

Question 36

Mark two answers

On a long motorway journey boredom can cause you to feel sleepy. You should

a leave the motorway and find a safe place to stop
b keep looking around at the surrounding landscape
c drive faster to complete your journey sooner
d ensure a supply of fresh air into your vehicle
e stop on the hard shoulder for a rest

Question 37

Mark one answer

In motorcycling, the term 'lifesaver' refers to

a a final, rearward glance
b an approved safety helmet
c a reflective jacket
d the two-second rule

Question 38

Mark two answers

You are driving at dusk. You should switch your lights on

a even when street lights are not lit
b so others can see you
c only when others have done so
d only when street lights are lit

Question 39

Mark one answer

Riding a motorcycle when you are cold could cause you to

a be more alert
b be more relaxed
c react more quickly
d lose concentration

Question 40

Mark one answer

Why are these yellow lines painted across the road?

a To help you choose the correct lane

b To help you keep the correct separation distance

c To make you aware of your speed

d To tell you the distance to the roundabout

Question 41

Mark one answer

You are riding at night and are dazzled by the lights of an approaching vehicle. What should you do?

a Switch off your headlight

b Switch to main beam

c Slow down and stop

d Flash your headlight

Question 42

Mark one answer

Which of the following should you do before stopping?

a Sound the horn

b Use the mirrors

c Select a higher gear

d Flash your headlights

Question 43

Mark one answer

You are approaching traffic lights that have been on green for some time. You should

a accelerate hard

b maintain your speed

c be ready to stop

d brake hard

Question 44

Mark three answers

When you are moving off from behind a parked car you should

a look round before you move off

b use all the mirrors on the vehicle

c look round after moving off

d use the exterior mirrors only

e give a signal if necessary

f give a signal after moving off

Answers and explanations

Q001 c

Q002 a Before moving off you should check over your right shoulder to make sure that no one is there who could not be seen in your mirrors.

Q003 b You must not use a hand-held telephone while you are driving.

Q004 c

Q005 b

Q006 d A motorcyclist or cyclist could be hidden in the blind area and not visible in your mirrors. A quick sideways glance before changing lanes ensures that it is safe.

Q007 d If it's a hand-held phone you must pull up before answering. If it's hands-free it is still advisable to stop.

Q008 c You should always check your blind spot just before moving off or starting a manoeuvre.

Q009 d

Q010 d

Q011 c Mirrors should be adjusted to give you the best view of the road behind. If your shoulders or elbows obstruct the view behind you should fit alternative mirrors with longer stems.

Q012 a, c

Q013 a, e

Q014 a, b

Q015 b

Q016 a, b, c, d

Q017 b

Q018 b This helps you maintain control of your car.

Q019 d

Q020 b, d, f

Q021 c

Q022 d

Q023 a, b, c, d

Q024 c

Q025 b

Q026 c

Q027 d You are not allowed to use a hand-held mobile phone whilst driving. Even a hands-free system can distract your attention from the road.

Q028 b

Q029 c

Q030 a

Answers and explanations

Q031   c

Q032   c Answering a mobile phone while driving might distract your attention. You should pull up first.

Q033   c

Q034   b

Q035   b

Q036   a, d

Q037   a

Q038   a, b

Q039   d

Q040   c

Q041   c

Q042   b

Q043   c

Q044   a, b, e

Theory Test Questions

2001/2002

Attitude

BSM

We won't fail you

Question 1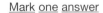

Mark one answer

You are approaching a zebra crossing. Pedestrians are waiting to cross. You should

a give way to the elderly and infirm only

b slow down and prepare to stop

c use your headlights to indicate they can cross

d wave at them to cross the road

Question 2

Mark one answer

You are driving a slow-moving vehicle on a narrow winding road. You should

a keep well out to stop vehicles overtaking dangerously

b wave following vehicles past you if you think they can overtake quickly

c pull in safely when you can, to let following vehicles overtake

d give a left signal when it is safe for vehicles to overtake you

Question 3

Mark one answer

You are driving a slow-moving vehicle on a narrow road. When traffic wishes to overtake you should

a take no action

b put your hazard warning lights on

c stop immediately and wave it on

d pull in safely as soon as you can do so

Question 4

Mark one answer

You are approaching a red light at a puffin crossing. Pedestrians are on the crossing. The red light will stay on until

a you start to edge forward on to the crossing

b the pedestrians have reached a safe position

c the pedestrians are clear of the front of your motorcycle

d a driver from the opposite direction reaches the crossing

Question 5

Mark one answer

You are driving a slow-moving vehicle on a narrow, winding road. In order to let other vehicles overtake you should

a wave to them to pass

b pull in when you can

c show a left-turn signal

d keep left and hold your speed

Question 6

Mark one answer

You are riding a slow-moving scooter on a narrow, winding road. You should

a keep well out to stop vehicles overtaking dangerously

b wave following vehicles past you if you think they can overtake quickly

c pull in safely when you can, to let following vehicles overtake

d give a left signal when it is safe for vehicles to overtake you

Question 7

Mark one answer

A vehicle pulls out in front of you at a junction. What should you do?

a Swerve past it and sound your horn

b Flash your headlights and drive up close behind

c Slow down and be ready to stop

d Accelerate past it immediately

Question 8

Mark one answer

You stop for pedestrians waiting to cross at a zebra crossing. They do not start to cross. What should you do?

a Be patient and wait

b Sound your horn

c Carry on

d Wave them to cross

Question 9

Mark one answer

You are travelling at the legal speed limit. A vehicle comes up quickly behind, flashing its headlights. You should

a accelerate to make a gap behind you

b touch the brakes sharply to show your brake lights

c maintain your speed to prevent the vehicle from overtaking

d allow the vehicle to overtake

Question 10

Mark one answer

A bus is stopped at a bus stop ahead of you. Its right-hand indicator is flashing. You should

a flash your headlights and slow down

b slow down and give way if it is safe to do so

c sound your horn and keep going

d slow down and then sound your horn

Question 11

Mark one answer

You are riding towards a zebra crossing. Pedestrians are waiting to cross. You should

a give way to the elderly and infirm only

b slow down and prepare to stop

c use your headlight to indicate they can cross

d wave at them to cross the road

Question 12

Mark one answer

You are following this lorry. You should keep well back from it to

a give you a good view of the road ahead

b stop following traffic from rushing through the junction

c prevent traffic behind you from overtaking

d allow you to hurry through the traffic lights if they change

Question 13

Mark one answer

You should ONLY flash your headlights to other road users

a to show that you are giving way

b to show that you are about to turn

c to tell them that you have right of way

d to let them know that you are there

Question 14

Mark one answer

You are approaching a red light at a puffin crossing. Pedestrians are on the crossing. The red light will stay on until

a you start to edge forward on to the crossing

b the pedestrians have reached a safe position

c the pedestrians are clear of the front of your vehicle

d a driver from the opposite direction reaches the crossing

Question 15

Mark one answer

A pelican crossing that crosses the road in a STRAIGHT line and has a central island MUST be treated as

a one crossing in daylight only

b one complete crossing

c two separate crossings

d two crossings during darkness

Question 16

Mark one answer

You are approaching a pelican crossing. The amber light is flashing. You must

a give way to pedestrians who are crossing

b encourage pedestrians to cross

c not move until the green light appears

d stop even if the crossing is clear

Question 17

Mark one answer

You are riding a motorcycle and following a large vehicle at 40mph. You should position yourself

a close behind to make it easier to overtake the vehicle

b to the left of the road to make it easier to be seen

c close behind the vehicle to keep out of the wind

d well back so that you can see past the vehicle

Question 18

Mark one answer

At puffin crossings which light will not show to a driver?

a Flashing amber

b Red

c Steady amber

d Green

Question 19

Mark one answer

You could use the 'Two-Second Rule'

a before restarting the engine after it has stalled

b to keep a safe gap from the vehicle in front

c before using the 'Mirror-Signal-Manoeuvre' routine

d when emerging on wet roads

Question 20

Mark one answer

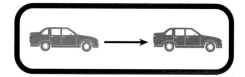

A two-second gap between yourself and the car in front is sufficient when conditions are

a wet

b good

c damp

d foggy

Question 21

Mark one answer

'Tailgating' means

a using the rear door of a hatchback car

b reversing into a parking space

c following another vehicle too closely

d driving with rear fog lights on

Question 22

Mark one answer

Scooter riders should be especially careful when crossing tram lines because scooters have

a small engines

b wide panniers

c automatic gear boxes

d narrow tyres

Question 23

Mark one answer

You are driving on a clear night. There is a steady stream of oncoming traffic. The national speed limit applies. Which lights should you use?

a Full beam headlights

b Sidelights

c Dipped headlights

d Fog lights

Question 24

Mark one answer

You are driving behind a large goods vehicle. It signals left but steers to the right. You should

a slow down and let the vehicle turn

b drive on, keeping to the left

c overtake on the right of it

d hold your speed and sound your horn

Question 25

Mark one answer

You are following a vehicle on a wet road. You should leave a time gap of at least

a one second

b two seconds

c three seconds

d four seconds

Question 26

Mark one answer

You are driving along this road. The red van cuts in close in front of you. What should you do?

a Accelerate to get closer to the red van

b Give a long blast on the horn

c Drop back to leave the correct separation distance

d Flash your headlights several times

Question 27

Mark one answer

You are waiting in a traffic queue at night. To avoid dazzling following drivers you should

a apply the handbrake only

b apply the footbrake only

c switch off your headlights

d use both the handbrake and footbrake

Question 28

Mark one answer

You are driving in traffic at the speed limit for the road. The driver behind is trying to overtake. You should

a move closer to the car ahead, so the driver behind has no room to overtake

b wave the driver behind to overtake when it is safe

c keep a steady course and allow the driver behind to overtake

d accelerate to get away from the driver behind

Question 29

Mark one answer

You are riding on a country road. Two horses with riders are in the distance. You should

a continue at your normal speed

b change down the gears quickly

c slow down and be ready to stop

d flash your headlight to warn them

Question 30

Mark one answer

You are driving at night on an unlit road following a slower-moving vehicle. You should

a flash your headlights

b use dipped beam headlights

c switch off your headlights

d use full beam headlights

Question 31

Mark one answer

A long, heavily-laden lorry is taking a long time to overtake you. What should you do?

a Speed up

b Slow down

c Hold your speed

d Change direction

Question 32

Mark three answers

Which THREE of these emergency services might have blue flashing beacons?

a Coastguard

b Bomb disposal

c Gritting lorries

d Animal ambulances

e Mountain rescue

f Doctors' cars

Question 33

Mark one answer

A flashing green beacon on a vehicle means

a police on non-urgent duties

b doctor on an emergency call

c road safety patrol operating

d gritting in progress

Question 34

Mark two answers

When riding a motorcycle your normal road position should allow

a other vehicles to overtake on your left

b the driver ahead to see you in the mirrors

c you to prevent following vehicles from overtaking

d you to be seen by traffic that is emerging from junctions ahead

e you to ride within half a metre (1 foot 8 ins) of the kerb

Question 35

Mark one answer

Diamond-shaped signs give instructions to

a tram drivers

b bus drivers

c lorry drivers

d taxi drivers

Question 36

Mark one answer

On a road where trams operate, which of these vehicles will be most at risk from the tram rails?

a Cars
b Cycles
c Buses
d Lorries

Question 37

Mark one answer

A bus lane on your left shows no times of operation. This means it is

a not in operation at all
b only in operation at peak times
c in operation 24 hours a day
d only in operation in daylight hours

Question 38

Mark one answer

What should you use your horn for?

a To alert others to your presence
b To allow you right of way
c To greet other road users
d To signal your annoyance

Question 39

Mark one answer

You are in a one-way street and want to turn right. You should position yourself

a in the right-hand lane
b in the left-hand lane
c in either lane, depending on the traffic
d just left of the centre line

Question 40

Mark one answer

You wish to turn right ahead. Why should you take up the correct position in good time?

a To allow other drivers to pull out in front of you
b To give a better view into the road that you're joining
c To help other road users know what you intend to do
d To allow drivers to pass you on the right

Question 41

Mark two answers

You are driving along a country road. A horse and rider are approaching. What should you do?

a Increase your speed
b Sound your horn
c Flash your headlights
d Drive slowly past
e Give plenty of room
f Rev your engine

Question 42

Mark one answer

A person herding sheep asks you to stop. You should

a ignore them as they have no authority

b stop and switch off your engine

c continue on but drive slowly

d try and get past quickly

Question 43

Mark one answer

When overtaking a horse and rider you should

a sound your horn as a warning

b go past as quickly as possible

c flash your headlights as a warning

d go past slowly and carefully

Question 44

Mark one answer

At a puffin crossing what colour follows the green signal?

a Steady red

b Flashing amber

c Steady amber

d Flashing green

Question 45

Mark one answer

You should never wave people across at pedestrian crossings because

a there may be another vehicle coming

b they may not be looking

c it is safer for you to carry on

d they may not be ready to cross

Question 46

Mark one answer

At a pelican crossing the flashing amber light means you MUST

a stop and wait for the green light

b stop and wait for the red light

c give way to pedestrians waiting to cross

d give way to pedestrians already on the crossing

Question 47

Mark one answer

Following this vehicle too closely is unwise because

a your brakes will overheat

b your view ahead is increased

c your engine will overheat

d your view ahead is reduced

Question 48

Mark one answer

You are in a line of traffic. The driver behind you is following very closely. What action should you take?

a Ignore the following driver and continue to drive within the speed limit

b Slow down, gradually increasing the gap between you and the vehicle in front

c Signal left and wave the following driver past

d Move over to a position just left of the centre line of the road

Question 49

Mark three answers

Which of the following vehicles will use blue flashing beacons?

a Motorway maintenance

b Bomb disposal

c Blood transfusion

d Police patrol

e Breakdown recovery

Question 50

Mark one answer

When being followed by an ambulance showing a flashing blue beacon you should

a pull over as soon as safely possible to let it pass

b accelerate hard to get away from it

c maintain your speed and course

d brake harshly and immediately stop in the road

Question 51

Mark one answer

What type of emergency vehicle is fitted with a green flashing beacon?

a Fire engine

b Road gritter

c Ambulance

d Doctor's car

Question 52

Mark one answer

A vehicle has a flashing green beacon. What does this mean?

a A doctor is answering an emergency call

b The vehicle is slow-moving

c It is a motorway police patrol vehicle

d A vehicle is carrying hazardous chemicals

Question 53

Mark one answer

At which type of crossing are cyclists allowed to ride across with pedestrians?

a Toucan

b Puffin

c Pelican

d Zebra

Answers and explanations

Q001 b

Q002 c 'a' and 'b' are dangerous and 'd' is confusing. Other drivers might think you are stopping or turning left.

Q003 d

Q004 b

Q005 b

Q006 c

Q007 c This is the only safe thing to do. The other answers are the actions of an aggressive driver.

Q008 a

Q009 d This is your only safe option.

Q010 b

Q011 b

Q012 a The nearer you are to a lorry, the less you can see ahead.

Q013 d You should only flash your headlights to warn other road users that you are there.

Q014 b

Q015 b

Q016 a You must give way to pedestrians already on the crossing but may drive on if the crossing is clear.

Q017 d If you can see past the vehicle you can decide whether it is safe to overtake.

Q018 a

Q019 b A two-second time gap from the vehicle in front provides a safe gap in good conditions.

Q020 b

Q021 c

Q022 d

Q023 c

Q024 a

Q025 d In good conditions you should allow two seconds but on a wet road you double this to four.

Q026 c

Q027 a Using the footbrake would activate your brake lights and might dazzle following drivers.

Q028 c

Q029 c Take extra care where there are horses around as they can easily be alarmed.

Q030 b

Q031 b By slowing down, you allow the lorry to get past, which is the only safe option.

Q032 a, b, e

Q033 b

Q034 b, d Motorcycles are easily missed by other road users. It is important that you make sure other drivers can see you.

Q035 a

Answers and explanations

Q036 b

Q037 c

Q038 a

Q039 a To turn right from a one-way street you normally position yourself in the right-hand lane.

Q040 c The position of your car helps signal your intentions to other drivers.

Q041 d, e

Q042 b

Q043 d

Q044 c

Q045 a

Q046 d

Q047 d If you hang back you will have a much better view of the road ahead.

Q048 b By increasing the gap between you and the vehicle in front, you give yourself and the driver behind more room to stop should you need it.

Q049 b, c, d

Q050 a

Q051 d Doctors on emergency call may display a flashing green beacon. Slow-moving vehicles have amber flashing beacons. Police, fire and ambulance service vehicles have blue flashing beacons.

Q052 a

Q053 a

Theory Test Questions

2001/2002

Safety & Your Vehicle

We won't fail you

Question 1

Mark one answer

How can you reduce the chances of your car being broken into when leaving it unattended?

a Take all contents with you

b Park near a taxi rank

c Place any valuables on the floor

d Park near a fire station

Question 2

Mark one answer

You have to leave valuables in your car. It would be safer to

a put them in a carrier bag

b park near a school entrance

c lock them out of sight

d park near a bus stop

Question 3

Mark one answer

How could you deter theft from your car when leaving it unattended?

a Leave valuables in a carrier bag

b Lock valuables out of sight

c Put valuables on the seats

d Leave valuables on the floor

Question 4

Mark one answer

Which of the following may help to deter a thief from stealing your car?

a Always keeping the headlights on

b Fitting reflective glass windows

c Always keeping the interior light on

d Etching the car number on the windows

Question 5

Mark one answer

How can you help to prevent your car radio being stolen?

a Park in an unlit area

b Hide the radio with a blanket

c Park near a busy junction

d Install a security coded radio

Question 6

Mark one answer

Which of the following should not be kept in your vehicle?

a A first aid kit

b A road atlas

c The tax disc

d The vehicle documents

Question 7

Mark one answer

What should you do when leaving your vehicle?

a Put valuable documents under the seats

b Remove all valuables

c Cover valuables with a blanket

d Leave the interior light on

Question 8

Mark one answer

You are parking your car. You have some valuables which you are unable to take with you. What should you do?

a Park near a police station

b Put them under the driver's seat

c Lock them out of sight

d Park in an unlit side road

Question 9

Mark one answer

Which of these is most likely to deter the theft of your vehicle?

a An immobiliser

b Tinted windows

c Locking wheel nuts

d A sun screen

Question 10

Mark one answer

Wherever possible, which one of the following should you do when parking at night?

a Park in a quiet car park

b Park in a well-lit area

c Park facing against the flow of traffic

d Park next to a busy junction

Question 11

Mark one answer

When parking and leaving your car you should

a park under a shady tree

b remove the tax disc

c park in a quiet road

d engage the steering lock

Question 12

Mark one answer

When leaving your vehicle parked and unattended you should

a park near a busy junction

b park in a housing estate

c remove the key and lock it

d leave the left indicator on

Question 13

Mark one answer

How can you lessen the risk of your vehicle being broken into at night?

a Leave it in a well-lit area

b Park in a quiet side road

c Don't engage the steering lock

d Park in a poorly lit area

Question 14

Mark one answer

To help keep your car secure you could join

a a vehicle breakdown organisation

b a vehicle watch scheme

c an advanced drivers scheme

d a car maintenance class

Question 15

Mark one answer

You forget to switch the choke off after the engine warms up. This could

a flatten the battery

b reduce braking distances

c use less fuel

d cause much more engine wear

Question 16

Mark one answer

When riding your motorcycle a tyre bursts. What should you do?

a Slow gently to a stop

b Brake firmly to a stop

c Change to a high gear

d Lower the side stand

Question 17

Mark one answer

A motorcycle engine that is properly maintained will

a use much more fuel

b have lower exhaust emissions

c increase your insurance premiums

d not need to have an MOT

Question 18

Mark one answer

An engine cut out switch should be used to

a reduce speed in an emergency

b prevent the motorcycle being stolen

c stop the engine normally

d stop the engine in an emergency

Question 19

Mark one answer

How often should motorcycle tyre pressures be checked?

a At least every two months

b After each long journey

c At least every two weeks

d Only at each regular service

Question 20

Mark one answer

What should you clean visors and goggles with?

a Petrol

b White spirit

c Antifreeze

d Soapy water

Question 21

Mark one answer

You are riding on a quiet road. Your visor fogs up. What should you do?

a Continue at a reduced speed

b Stop as soon as possible and wipe it

c Build up speed to increase air flow

d Close the helmet air vents

Question 22

Mark one answer

You are riding in hot weather. What is the safest type of footwear?

a Sandals

b Trainers

c Shoes

d Boots

Question 23

Mark one answer

A friend offers you a second-hand safety helmet for you to use. Why may this be a bad idea?

a It may be damaged

b You will be breaking the law

c You will affect your insurance cover

d It may be a full face type

Question 24

Mark one answer

Which of the following should not be used to fasten your safety helmet?

a Double D-ring fastening

b Velcro tab

c Quick release fastening

d Bar and buckle

Question 25

Mark one answer

After warming up the engine you leave the choke ON. What will this do?

a Discharge the battery

b Use more fuel

c Improve handling

d Use less fuel

Question 26

Mark one answer

Rear facing baby seats should NEVER be used on a seat protected with

a an airbag

b seat belts

c head restraints

d seat covers

Question 27

Mark two answers

You want to ride your motorcycle in the dark. What could you wear to be seen more easily?

a A black leather jacket

b Reflective clothing

c A white helmet

d A red helmet

Question 28

Mark one answer

It is essential that tyre pressures are checked regularly. When should this be done?

a After any lengthy journey

b After travelling at high speed

c When tyres are hot

d When tyres are cold

Question 29

Mark one answer

When should you NOT use your horn in a built-up area?

a Between 8 pm and 8 am

b Between 9 pm and dawn

c Between dusk and 8 am

d Between 11.30 pm and 7 am

Question 30

Mark four answers

You are riding a motorcycle of more than 50cc. Which FOUR would make a tyre illegal?

a Tread less than 1.6 mm deep

b Tread less than 1 mm deep

c A large bulge in the wall

d A recut tread

e Exposed ply or cord

f A stone wedged in the tread

Question 31

Mark one answer

Why are mirrors often slightly curved (convex)?

a They give a wider field of vision

b They totally cover blind spots

c They make it easier to judge the speed of following traffic

d They make following traffic look bigger

Question 32

Mark two answers

You should maintain cable-operated brakes

a by regular adjustment when necessary

b at normal service times only

c yearly, before taking the motorcycle for its MOT

d by oiling cables and pivots regularly

Question 33

Mark two answers

Which TWO of the following will improve fuel consumption?

a Reducing your road speed

b Planning well ahead

c Late and harsh braking

d Driving in lower gears

e Short journeys with a cold engine

f Rapid acceleration

Question 34

Mark one answer

Why can it be helpful to have mirrors fitted on each side of your motorcycle?

a To judge the gap when filtering in traffic

b To give protection when riding in poor weather

c To make your motorcycle appear larger to other drivers

d To give you the best view of the road behind

Question 35

Mark two answers

For which TWO of these may you use hazard warning lights?

a When driving on a motorway, to warn drivers behind of a hazard ahead

b When you are double parked on a two-way road

c When your direction indicators are not working

d When warning oncoming traffic that you intend to stop

e When your vehicle has broken down and is causing an obstruction

Question 36

Mark three answers

A motorcyclist may only carry a pillion passenger when

a the rider has successfully completed CBT (Compulsory Basic Training)

b the rider holds a full licence for the category of motorcycle

c the motorcycle is fitted with rear foot pegs

d the rider has a full car licence and is over 21

e there is a proper passenger seat fitted

f there is no sidecar fitted to the machine

Question 37

Mark one answer

Why do MOT tests include a strict exhaust emission test?

a To recover the cost of expensive garage equipment

b To help protect the environment against pollution

c To discover which fuel supplier is used the most

d To make sure diesel and petrol engines emit the same fumes

Question 38

Mark one answer

Which of these, if allowed to get low, could cause an accident?

a Antifreeze level

b Brake fluid level

c Battery water level

d Radiator coolant level

Question 39

Mark one answer

Your vehicle/motorcycle has a catalytic converter. Its purpose is to reduce

a exhaust noise

b fuel consumption

c exhaust emissions

d engine noise

Question 40

What is most likely to cause high fuel consumption?

a Poor steering control
b Accelerating around bends
c Staying in high gears
d Harsh braking and accelerating

Question 41

A properly serviced vehicle will give

a lower insurance premiums
b you a refund on your road tax
c better fuel economy
d cleaner exhaust emissions

Question 42

When riding a different motorcycle you should

a ask someone to ride with you for the first time
b ride as soon as possible as all controls and switches are the same
c leave your gloves behind so switches can be operated easier at first
d be sure you know where all controls and switches are

Question 43

You enter a road where there are road humps. What should you do?

a Maintain a reduced speed throughout
b Accelerate quickly between each one
c Always keep to the maximum legal speed
d Drive slowly at school times only

Question 44

When should you especially check the engine oil level?

a Before a long journey
b When the engine is hot
c Early in the morning
d Every 6,000 miles

Question 45

Mark one answer

A loose drive chain on a motorcycle could cause

a the front wheel to wobble

b the ignition to cut out

c the brakes to fail

d the rear wheel to lock

Question 46

Mark four answers

Which FOUR of these MUST be in good working order for your car to be roadworthy?

a Temperature gauge

b Speedometer

c Windscreen washers

d Windscreen wiper

e Oil warning light

f Horn

Question 47

Mark three answers

A wrongly-adjusted drive chain can

a cause an accident

b make wheels wobble

c create a noisy rattle

d affect gear changing

e cause a suspension fault

Question 48

Mark three answers

Which THREE does the law require you to keep in good condition?

a Gears

b Transmission

c Headlights

d Windscreen

e Seat belts

Question 49

Mark one answer

New petrol-engined cars must be fitted with catalytic converters. The reason for this is to

a control exhaust noise levels

b prolong the life of the exhaust system

c allow the exhaust system to be recycled

d reduce harmful exhaust emissions

Question 50

Mark one answer

What is the most important reason why you should keep your motorcycle regularly maintained?

a To accelerate faster than other traffic

b So the motorcycle can carry panniers

c To keep the machine roadworthy

d So the motorcycle can carry a passenger

Question 51

Mark two answers

Which TWO are badly affected if the tyres are under-inflated?

a Braking

b Steering

c Changing gear

d Parking

Question 52

Mark one answer

The legal minimum depth of tread for motorcycle tyres is

a 1 mm

b 1.6 mm

c 2.5 mm

d 4 mm

Question 53

Mark one answer

What can cause heavy steering?

a Driving on ice

b Badly worn brakes

c Over-inflated tyres

d Under-inflated tyres

Question 54

Mark one answer

Your motorcycle has tubed tyres fitted as standard. When replacing a tyre you should

a replace the tube if it is 6 months old

b replace the tube if it has covered 6,000 miles

c replace the tube only if replacing the rear tyre

d replace the tube with each change of tyre

Question 55

Mark two answers

Driving with under-inflated tyres can affect

a engine temperature

b fuel consumption

c braking

d oil pressure

Question 56

Mark one answer

How should you ride a motorcycle when NEW tyres have just been fitted?

a Carefully, until the shiny surface is worn off

b By braking hard especially into bends

c Through normal riding with higher air pressures

d By riding at faster than normal speeds

Question 57

Mark one answer

It is illegal to drive with tyres that

a have been bought second-hand

b have a large deep cut in the side wall

c are of different makes

d are of different tread patterns

Question 58

Mark one answer

The legal minimum depth of tread for car tyres over three quarters of the breadth is

a 1 mm

b 1.6 mm

c 2.5 mm

d 4 mm

Question 59

Mark two answers

Excessive or uneven tyre wear can be caused by faults in the

a gearbox

b braking system

c suspension

d exhaust system

Question 60

Mark one answer

Which of the following would NOT make you more visible in daylight?

a A black helmet

b A white helmet

c Switching on your dipped headlamp

d Wearing a fluorescent jacket

Question 61

Mark one answer

Your vehicle pulls to one side when braking. You should

a change the tyres around

b consult your garage as soon as possible

c pump the pedal when braking

d use your handbrake at the same time

Question 62

Mark one answer

When riding and wearing brightly coloured clothing you will

a dazzle other motorists on the road

b be seen more easily by other motorists

c create a hazard by distracting other drivers

d be able to ride on unlit roads at night with sidelights

Question 63

Mark one answer

The main cause of brake fade is

a the brakes overheating

b air in the brake fluid

c oil on the brakes

d the brakes out of adjustment

Question 64

Mark one answer

You are riding a motorcycle in very hot weather. You should

a ride with your visor fully open

b continue to wear protective clothing

c wear trainers instead of boots

d slacken your helmet strap

Question 65

Mark one answer

Your anti-lock brakes warning light stays on. You should

a check the brake fluid level

b check the footbrake free play

c check that the handbrake is released

d have the brakes checked immediately

Question 66

Mark one answer

Why should you wear fluorescent clothing when riding in daylight?

a It reduces wind resistance

b It prevents injury if you come off the machine

c It helps other road users to see you

d It keeps you cool in hot weather

Question 67

Mark one answer

What does this instrument panel light mean when lit?

a Gear lever in park

b Gear lever in neutral

c Handbrake on

d Handbrake off

Question 68

Mark one answer

Why should riders wear reflective clothing?

a To protect them from the cold

b To protect them from direct sunlight

c To be seen better in daylight

d To be seen better at night

Question 69

Mark one answer

When MUST you use dipped headlights during the day?

a All the time

b Along narrow streets

c In poor visibility

d When parking

Question 70

Mark three answers

Which of the following make it easier for motorcyclists to be seen?

a Using a dipped headlight

b Wearing a fluorescent jacket

c Wearing a white helmet

d Wearing a grey helmet

e Wearing black leathers

f Using a tinted visor

Question 71

Mark one answer

Which instrument panel warning light would show that headlights are on full beam?

 a   **b**

 c   **d**

Question 72

Mark one answer

While driving, this warning light on your dashboard comes on. It means

a a fault in the braking system

b the engine oil is low

c a rear light has failed

d your seat belt is not fastened

Question 73

Mark one answer

Which of the following fairings would give you the best weather protection?

a Handlebar

b Sports

c Touring

d Windscreen

Question 74

Mark one answer

You are driving on a motorway. The traffic ahead is braking sharply because of an accident. How could you warn following traffic?

a Briefly use the hazard warning lights

b Switch on the hazard warning lights continuously

c Briefly use the rear fog lights

d Switch on the headlights continuously

Question 75

Mark one answer

It would be illegal to ride WITH a helmet on when

a the helmet is not fastened correctly

b the helmet is more than four years old

c you have borrowed someone else's helmet

d the helmet does not have chin protection

Question 76

Mark one answer

When may you use hazard warning lights?

a To park alongside another car

b To park on double yellow lines

c When you are being towed

d When you have broken down

Question 77

Mark one answer

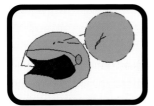

Your safety helmet has a small crack. You should

a get a new one before riding

b ride at low speeds only

c ask the police to inspect it

d have it repaired by an expert

Question 78

Mark one answer

Hazard warning lights should be used when vehicles are

a broken down and causing an obstruction

b faulty and moving slowly

c being towed along a road

d reversing into a side road

Question 79

Mark one answer

Your visor becomes badly scratched. You should

a polish it with a fine abrasive

b replace it

c wash it in soapy water

d clean it with petrol

Question 80

Mark one answer

It is important to wear suitable shoes when you are driving. Why is this?

a To prevent wear on the pedals

b To maintain control of the pedals

c To enable you to adjust your seat

d To enable you to walk for assistance if you break down

Question 81

Mark <u>one</u> <u>answer</u>

A properly adjusted head restraint will

a make you more comfortable

b help you to avoid neck injury

c help you to relax

d help you to maintain your driving position

Question 82

Mark <u>one</u> <u>answer</u>

When MUST you use a dipped headlight during the day?

a On country roads

b In poor visibility

c Along narrow streets

d When parking

Question 83

Mark <u>one</u> <u>answer</u>

What will reduce the risk of neck injury resulting from a collision?

a An air-sprung seat

b Anti-lock brakes

c A collapsible steering wheel

d A properly adjusted head restraint

Question 84

Mark <u>two</u> <u>answers</u>

A properly serviced motorcycle will give

a lower insurance premiums

b you a refund on your road tax

c better fuel economy

d cleaner exhaust emission

Question 85

Mark <u>three</u> <u>answers</u>

How can you, as a driver, help the environment?

a By reducing your speed

b By gentle acceleration

c By using leaded fuel

d By driving faster

e By harsh acceleration

f By servicing your vehicle properly

Question 86

Mark <u>three</u> <u>answers</u>

To help the environment, you can avoid wasting fuel by

a having your vehicle properly serviced

b ensuring your tyres are correctly inflated

c not over-revving in the lower gears

d driving at higher speeds where possible

e keeping an empty roof rack properly fitted

f servicing your vehicle less regularly

Question 87

<u>Mark</u> <u>three</u> <u>answers</u>

Which THREE things can you, as a road user, do to help the environment?

a Cycle when possible

b Drive on under-inflated tyres

c Use the choke for as long as possible on a cold engine

d Have your vehicle properly tuned and serviced

e Watch the traffic and plan ahead

f Brake as late as possible without skidding

Question 88

<u>Mark</u> <u>three</u> <u>answers</u>

As a driver you can cause MORE damage to the environment by

a choosing a fuel efficient vehicle

b making a lot of short journeys

c driving in as high a gear as possible

d accelerating as quickly as possible

e having your vehicle regularly serviced

f using leaded fuel

Question 89

<u>Mark</u> <u>three</u> <u>answers</u>

Motor vehicles can harm the environment. This has resulted in

a air pollution

b damage to buildings

c reduced health risks

d improved public transport

e less use of electrical vehicles

f using up natural resources

Question 90

<u>Mark</u> <u>three</u> <u>answers</u>

To reduce the damage your vehicle causes to the environment you should

a use narrow side streets

b avoid harsh acceleration

c brake in good time

d anticipate well ahead

e use busy routes

Question 91

<u>Mark</u> <u>one</u> <u>answer</u>

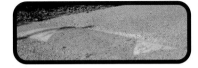

You enter a road where there are road humps. What should you do?

a Maintain a reduced speed throughout

b Accelerate quickly between each one

c Always keep to the maximum legal speed

d Ride slowly at school times only

Question 92

Mark one answer

To help protect the environment you should NOT

a remove your roof rack when unloaded

b use your car for very short journeys

c walk, cycle, or use public transport

d empty the boot of unnecessary weight

Question 93

Mark one answer

Tyre pressures should be increased on your motorcycle when

a riding on a wet road

b carrying a pillion passenger

c travelling on an uneven surface

d riding on twisty roads

Question 94

Mark one answer

You service your own vehicle. How should you get rid of the old engine oil?

a Take it to a local authority site

b Pour it down a drain

c Tip it into a hole in the ground

d Put it into your dustbin

Question 95

Mark one answer

Your oil light comes on as you are riding. You should

a go to a dealer for an oil change

b go to the nearest garage for their advice

c ride slowly for a few miles to see if the light goes out

d stop as quickly as possible and try to find the cause

Question 96

Mark one answer

You are carrying two 13-year-old children and their parents in your car. Who is responsible for seeing that the children wear seat belts?

a The children's parents

b You, the driver

c The front-seat passenger

d The children

Question 97

Mark three answers

When may you have to increase the tyre pressures on your motorcycle?

a When carrying a pillion passenger

b After a long journey

c When carrying heavy loads

d When riding at high speeds

e When riding in hot weather

Question 98

Mark one answer

You are driving a friend's children home from school. They are both under 14 years old. Who is responsible for making sure they wear a seat belt?

a An adult passenger

b The children

c You, the driver

d Your friend

Question 99

Mark two answers

Which TWO of these items on a motorcycle MUST be kept clean?

a Number plate

b Wheels

c Engine

d Fairing

e Headlights

Question 100

Mark one answer

Car passengers MUST wear a seat belt if one is available, unless they are

a under 14 years old

b under 1.5 metres (5 feet) in height

c sitting in the rear seat

d exempt for medical reasons

Question 101

Mark two answers

Motorcycle tyres MUST

a have the same tread pattern

b be correctly inflated

c be the same size, front and rear

d both be the same make

e have sufficient tread depth

Question 102

Mark three answers

Excessive or uneven tyre wear can be caused by faults in which THREE?

a The gearbox

b The braking system

c The accelerator

d The exhaust system

e Wheel alignment

f The suspension

Question 103

Mark one answer

You are riding on a wet road. When braking you should

a apply the rear brake well before the front

b apply the front brake just before the rear

c avoid using the front brake at all

d avoid using the rear brake at all

Question 104

Mark one answer

You are testing your suspension. You notice that your vehicle keeps bouncing when you press down on the front wing. What does this mean?

a Worn tyres

b Tyres under-inflated

c Steering wheel not located centrally

d Worn shock absorbers

Question 105

Mark one answer

You should use the engine cut-out switch on your motorcycle to

a save wear and tear on the battery

b stop the engine on short stops

c stop the engine in an emergency

d save wear and tear on the ignition

Question 106

Mark three answers

Which THREE of the following are most likely to waste fuel?

a Reducing your speed

b Carrying unnecessary weight

c Using the wrong grade of fuel

d Under-inflated tyres

e Using different brands of fuel

f A fitted, empty roof rack

Question 107

Mark one answer

Riding your motorcycle with a slack or worn drive chain may cause

a an engine misfire

b early tyre wear

c increased emissions

d a locked wheel

Question 108

Mark two answers

You have a loose filler cap on your diesel fuel tank. This will

a waste fuel and money

b make roads slippery for other road users

c improve your vehicle's fuel consumption

d increase the level of exhaust emissions

Question 109

Mark one answer

You have adjusted the drive chain tension. You should check the

a rear wheel alignment

b tyre pressures

c valve clearances

d sidelights

Question 110

Mark one answer

To avoid spillage after refuelling, you should make sure that

a your tank is only ³/₄ full

b you have used a locking filler cap

c you check your fuel gauge is working

d your filler cap is securely fastened

Question 111

Mark one answer

Extra care should be taken when refuelling, because diesel fuel when spilt is

a sticky

b odourless

c clear

d slippery

Question 112

Mark one answer

You must NOT sound your horn

a between 10 pm and 6 am in a built-up area

b at any time in a built-up area

c between 11.30 pm and 7 am in a built-up area

d between 11.30 pm and 6 am on any road

Question 113

Mark one answer

You cannot see clearly behind when reversing. What should you do?

a Open your window to look behind

b Open the door and look behind

c Look in the nearside mirror

d Ask someone to guide you

Question 114

Mark one answer

Driving at 70 mph uses more fuel than driving at 50 mph by up to

a 10%

b 30%

c 75%

d 100%

Question 115

Mark one answer

When driving a car fitted with automatic transmission what would you use 'kick down' for?

a Cruise control

b Quick acceleration

c Slow braking

d Fuel economy

Question 116

Mark one answer

When a roof rack is not in use it should be removed. Why is this?

a It will affect the suspension

b It is illegal

c It will affect your braking

d It will waste fuel

Question 117

Mark one answer

A roof rack fitted to your car will

a reduce fuel consumption

b improve the road handling

c make your car go faster

d increase fuel consumption

Question 118

Mark three answers

The pictured vehicle is 'environmentally friendly' because it

a reduces noise pollution

b uses diesel fuel

c uses electricity

d uses unleaded fuel

e reduces parking spaces

f reduces town traffic

Question 119

Mark one answer

Supertrams or Light Rapid Transit (LRT) systems are environmentally friendly because

a they use diesel power

b they use quieter roads

c they use electric power

d they do not operate during rush hour

Question 120

Mark one answer

'Red routes' in major cities have been introduced to

a raise the speed limits

b help the traffic flow

c provide better parking

d allow lorries to load more freely

Question 121

Mark three answers

To reduce the volume of traffic on the roads you could

a use public transport more often

b share a car when possible

c walk or cycle on short journeys

d travel by car at all times

e use a car with a smaller engine

f drive in a bus lane

Question 122

Mark one answer

In some narrow residential streets you will find a speed limit of

a 20 mph

b 25 mph

c 35 mph

d 40 mph

Question 123

Mark one answer

Road humps, chicanes, narrowings are

a always at major road works

b used to increase traffic speed

c at toll-bridge approaches only

d traffic calming measures

Question 124

Mark one answer

On your vehicle, where would you find a catalytic converter?

a In the fuel tank

b In the air filter

c On the cooling system

d On the exhaust system

Question 125

Mark one answer

Daytime visibility is poor but not seriously reduced. You should switch on

a headlights and fog lights

b front fog lights

c dipped headlights

d rear fog lights

Question 126

Mark one answer

Why are vehicles fitted with rear fog lights?

a To be seen when driving at high speed

b To use if broken down in a dangerous position

c To make them more visible in thick fog

d To warn drivers following closely to drop back

Question 127

Mark one answer

As a driver you can help reduce pollution levels in town centres by

a driving more quickly

b using leaded fuel

c walking or cycling

d driving short journeys

Question 128

Mark one answer

You will use more fuel if your tyres are

a under-inflated

b of different makes

c over-inflated

d new and hardly used

Question 129

Mark <u>two</u> <u>answers</u>

How should you dispose of a used battery?

a Take it to a local authority site

b Put it in the dustbin

c Break it up into pieces

d Leave it on waste land

e Take it to a garage

f Burn it on a fire

Question 130

Mark <u>one</u> <u>answer</u>

The purpose of a catalytic converter is to reduce

a fuel consumption

b the risk of fire

c toxic exhaust gases

d engine wear

Question 131

Mark <u>one</u> <u>answer</u>

Unbalanced wheels on a car may cause

a the steering to pull to one side

b the steering to vibrate

c the brakes to fail

d the tyres to deflate

Question 132

Mark <u>two</u> <u>answers</u>

Turning the steering wheel while your car is stationary can cause damage to the

a gearbox

b engine

c brakes

d steering

e tyres

Question 133

Mark <u>one</u> <u>answer</u>

Catalytic converters are fitted to make the

a engine produce more power

b exhaust system easier to replace

c engine run quietly

d exhaust fumes cleaner

Answers and explanations

Q001 a Your car is more likely to be broken into if valuables are visible through the windows.

Q002 c

Q003 b

Q004 d Would-be thieves may well be able to steal any vehicle but if your vehicle is secured, and preferably alarmed or immobilised, they may leave it alone.

Q005 d

Q006 d

Q007 b

Q008 c

Q009 a An anti-theft device like an immobiliser makes it more difficult for the would-be thief to steal your car.

Q010 b

Q011 d

Q012 c

Q013 a Avoid leaving your car unattended in poorly lit areas, especially if they are known to be high risk.

Q014 b

Q015 d As soon as the engine warms up remember to push in the manual choke, otherwise the engine could be damaged and petrol will be wasted.

Q016 a With emergencies of this nature avoid sudden braking or changes of direction.

Q017 b

Q018 d This switch only isolates the engine. Lights, if in use, will remain on.

Q019 c

Q020 d Most other cleaning agents may have a solvent content, which will damage the visor.

Q021 b

Q022 d Whatever the weather conditions, full safety clothing should always be worn.

Q023 a

Q024 b Velcro is only designed to tidy up more secure fastenings and would not be safe in an accident.

Q025 b

Q026 a The impact of the airbag, released in an accident, could kill a baby in a rear facing baby seat.

Q027 b, c

Answers and explanations

Q028 d With emergencies of this nature avoid sudden braking or changes of direction.

Q029 d

Q030 b, c, d, e

Q031 a Convex mirrors give a wider field of vision but also make traffic look further away than it really is, so you need to use them with care.

Q032 a, d

Q033 a, b

Q034 d

Q035 a, e

Q036 b, c, e

Q037 b

Q038 b A low level of brake fluid may cause your brakes to fail.

Q039 c

Q040 d Harsh braking is one of the major causes of high fuel consumption.

Q041 c, d

Q042 d

Q043 a Road humps are there to slow the traffic in residential areas.

Q044 a

Q045 d Drive chains require frequent adjustment and lubrication. If the chain is loose it can jump off the sprocket and lock the rear wheel.

Q046 b, c, d, f
These must, by law, be in good working order.

Q047 a, c, d

Q048 c, d, e

Q049 d This helps the car operate more efficiently and cause less air pollution. Only unleaded fuel may be used.

Q050 c

Q051 a, b

Q052 a

Q053 d

Q054 d A punctured tyre should be properly repaired or replaced and if you have tubed tyres this means replacing the inner tyre as well.

Q055 b, c

Q056 a New tyres have a shiny surface which can reduce the grip. You need to ride carefully until the shiny surface is worn off. This could take up to 100 miles.

Q057 b

Answers and explanations

Q058 b

Q059 b, c

Q060 a

Q061 b

Q062 b

Q063 a

Q064 b Protective clothing offers some kind of protection against injury in the event of an accident.

Q065 d

Q066 c

Q067 c

Q068 d

Q069 c

Q070 a, b, c

Q071 a

Q072 a

Q073 c

Q074 a

Q075 a

Q076 d You should not use hazard warning lights when being towed so 'c' is wrong.

Q077 a

Q078 a

Q079 b A badly scratched visor can distort your vision, causing dazzle from oncoming headlights at night and glare from a low winter sun.

Q080 b

Q081 b

Q082 b

Q083 d If you are involved in an accident, the head restraint helps protect your neck from whiplash.

Q084 c, d

Q085 a, b, f

Q086 a, b, c

Q087 a, d, e

Q088 b, d, f A lot of short journeys use up a lot of petrol and pollute the atmosphere with the exhaust fumes.

Q089 a, b, f

Q090 b, c, d Doing these make for smoother driving which uses less fuel and so cuts down on pollution.

Q091 a

Q092 b

Q093 b Inflate the tyres according to the maker's instruction.

Q094 a

Q095 d

Q096 b

Q097 a, c, d

Q098 c

Answers and explanations

Q099 a, e

Q100 d All passengers, front and
rear, must wear seat belts, if
fitted, unless exempt for
medical reasons.

Q101 b, e

Q102 b, e, f

Q103 b You need to apply a more
equal pressure to the front
and rear brakes than you
would in good road and
weather conditions.

Q104 d

Q105 c

Q106 b, d, f

Q107 d

Q108 a, b

Q109 a

Q110 d

Q111 d

Q112 c The regulation only applies in
a built up area.

Q113 d If you cannot see properly you
need to get someone to help.

Q114 b

Q115 b A short, firm pressure
right down on the gas pedal
causes a quick change down
to the next lower gear –
useful, for example, when
you need to overtake.

Q116 d

Q117 d

Q118 a, c, f

Q119 c

Q120 b

Q121 a, b, c

Q122 a This is a traffic calming
measure.

Q123 d

Q124 d

Q125 c If visibility drops below
about 100 metres (328 feet)
use fog lights.

Q126 c

Q127 c

Q128 a

Q129 a, e

Q130 c

Q131 b

Q132 d, e

Q133 d

Theory
Test
Questions

2001/2002

Safety Margins

BSM
We won't fail you

Question 1

Mark <u>one</u> <u>answer</u>

You are driving along a wet road. How can you tell if your vehicle's tyres are losing their grip on the surface?

a The engine will stall

b The steering will feel very heavy

c The engine noise will increase

d The steering will feel very light

Question 2

Mark <u>one</u> <u>answer</u>

You are riding in heavy rain. Why should you try to avoid this marked area?

a It is illegal to ride over bus stops

b The painted lines may be slippery

c Cyclists may be using the bus stop

d Only emergency vehicles may drive over bus stops

Question 3

Mark <u>one</u> <u>answer</u>

You are on a good, dry road surface and your vehicle has good brakes and tyres. What is the overall stopping distance at 40 mph?

a 23 metres (75 feet)

b 36 metres (118 feet)

c 53 metres (175 feet)

d 96 metres (315 feet)

Question 4

Mark <u>one</u> <u>answer</u>

Why should you try to avoid riding over this marked area?

a It is illegal to ride over bus stops

b It will alter your machine's centre of gravity

c Pedestrians may be waiting at the bus stop

d A bus may have left oil patches

Question 5

Mark one answer

What is the shortest stopping distance at 70 mph?

a 53 metres (175 feet)

b 60 metres (197 feet)

c 73 metres (240 feet)

d 96 metres (315 feet)

Question 6

Mark one answer

After riding through deep water you notice your scooter brakes do not work properly. What would be the best way to dry them out?

a Ride slowly, braking lightly

b Ride quickly, braking harshly

c Stop and dry them with a cloth

d Stop and wait for a few minutes

Question 7

Mark one answer

What is the shortest overall stopping distance on a dry road from 60 mph?

a 53 metres (175 feet)

b 58 metres (190 feet)

c 73 metres (240 feet)

d 96 metres (315 feet)

Question 8

Mark one answer

When riding at night you should

a wear reflective clothing

b wear a tinted visor

c ride in the middle of the road

d always give arm signals

Question 9

Mark one answer

Your indicators may be difficult to see in bright sunlight. What should you do?

a Put your indicator on earlier

b Give an arm signal as well as using your indicator

c Touch the brake several times to show the stop lights

d Turn as quickly as you can

Question 10

Mark one answer

When riding in extremely cold conditions what can you do to keep warm?

a Stay close to the vehicles in front
b Wear suitable clothing
c Lie flat on the tank
d Put one hand on the exhaust pipe

Question 11

Mark one answer

You are travelling at 50 mph on a good, dry road. What is your shortest overall stopping distance?

a 36 metres (120 feet)
b 53 metres (175 feet)
c 75 metres (245 feet)
d 96 metres (315 feet)

Question 12

Mark two answers

You are riding at night. To be seen more easily you should

a ride with your headlight on dipped beam
b wear reflective clothing
c keep the motorcycle clean
d stay well out to the right
e wear waterproof clothing

Question 13

Mark one answer

Your overall stopping distance will be much longer when driving

a in the rain
b in fog
c at night
d in strong winds

Question 14

Mark one answer

You have driven through a flood. What is the first thing you should do?

a Stop and check the tyres
b Stop and dry the brakes
c Check your exhaust
d Test your brakes

Question 15

Mark two answers

In very hot weather the road surface can get soft. Which TWO of the following will be affected most?

a The suspension
b The steering
c The braking
d The exhaust

Question 16

Mark one answer

When approaching a right-hand bend you should keep well to the left.
Why is this?

a To improve your view of the road
b To overcome the effect of the road's slope
c To let faster traffic from behind overtake
d To be positioned safely if you skid

Question 17

Mark three answers

You should not overtake when

a intending to turn left shortly afterwards
b in a one-way street
c approaching a junction
d going up a long hill
e the view ahead is blocked

Question 18

Mark one answer

Your overall stopping distance will be much longer when riding

a in the rain
b in fog
c at night
d in strong winds

Question 19

Mark one answer

You are on a good, dry road surface. Your vehicle has good brakes and tyres. What is the BRAKING distance at 50 mph?

a 38 metres (125 feet)
b 14 metres (46 feet)
c 24 metres (79 feet)
d 55 metres (180 feet)

Question 20

Mark two answers

You are riding in very hot weather. What are TWO effects that melting tar has on the control of your motorcycle?

a It can make the surface slippery
b It can reduce tyre grip
c It can reduce stopping distances
d It can improve braking efficiency

Question 21

Mark one answer

Your vehicle is fitted with anti-lock brakes. To stop quickly in an emergency you should

a brake firmly and pump the brake pedal on and off
b brake rapidly and firmly without releasing the brake pedal
c brake gently and pump the brake pedal on and off
d brake rapidly once, and immediately release the brake pedal

Question 22

Mark one answer

You are on a good, dry road surface and your motorcycle has good brakes and tyres. What is the overall stopping distance at 40 mph?

a 23 metres (75 feet)

b 36 metres (118 feet)

c 53 metres (175 feet)

d 96 metres (315 feet)

Question 23

Mark one answer

Your car is fitted with anti-lock brakes. You need to stop in an emergency. You should

a brake normally and avoid turning the steering wheel

b press the brake pedal rapidly and firmly until you have stopped

c keep pushing and releasing the foot brake quickly to prevent skidding

d apply the handbrake to reduce the stopping distance

Question 24

Mark one answer

You are on a good, dry road surface. Your motorcycle has good brakes and tyres. What is the BRAKING distance at 50 mph?

a 38 metres (125 feet)

b 14 metres (46 feet)

c 24 metres (79 feet)

d 55 metres (180 feet)

Question 25

Mark one answer

You are driving a vehicle fitted with anti-lock brakes. You need to stop in an emergency. You should apply the footbrake

a slowly and gently

b slowly but firmly

c rapidly and gently

d rapidly and firmly

Question 26

Mark one answer

Anti-lock brakes reduce the chances of a skid occurring particularly when

a driving down steep hills

b braking during normal driving

c braking in an emergency

d driving on good road surfaces

Question 27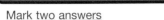

Mark two answers

Your vehicle has anti-lock brakes, but they may not always prevent skidding. This is most likely to happen when driving

a in foggy conditions

b on surface water

c on loose road surfaces

d on dry tarmac

e at night on unlit roads

Question 28

Mark one answer

Your overall stopping distance will be longer when riding

a at night

b in the fog

c with a passenger

d up a hill

Question 29

Mark one answer

Anti-lock brakes prevent wheels from locking. This means the tyres are less likely to

a aquaplane

b skid

c puncture

d wear

Question 30

Mark one answer

'Only a fool breaks the Two-Second Rule' refers to

a the time recommended when using the choke

b the separation distance when riding in good conditions

c restarting a stalled engine in busy traffic

d the time you should keep your foot down at a junction

Question 31

Mark one answer

Anti-lock brakes are most effective when you

a keep pumping the foot brake to prevent skidding

b brake normally, but grip the steering wheel tightly

c brake rapidly and firmly until you have slowed down

d apply the handbrake to reduce the stopping distance

Question 32

Mark one answer

On a wet road what is the safest way to stop?

a Change gear without braking

b Use the back brake only

c Use the front brake only

d Use both brakes

Question 33

Mark one answer

Vehicles fitted with anti-lock brakes

a are impossible to skid

b can be steered while you are braking

c accelerate much faster

d are not fitted with a handbrake

Question 34

Mark one answer

The road surface is very important to motorcyclists because

a there can be many areas where road markings are poor

b some roads are tarmac and others concrete

c as traffic increases there is less room for riders

d only a small part of the tyre touches the road

Question 35

Mark two answers

Anti-lock brakes may not work as effectively if the road surface is

a dry

b loose

c wet

d good

e firm

Question 36

Mark four answers

The road surface is very important to motorcyclists. Which FOUR of these are more likely to reduce the stability of your motorcycle?

a Potholes

b Drain covers

c Concrete

d Oil patches

e Tarmac

f Loose gravel

Question 37

Mark one answer

Anti-lock brakes are of most use when you are

a braking gently

b driving on worn tyres

c braking excessively

d driving normally

Question 38

Mark one answer

You are riding in town at night. The roads are wet after rain. The reflections from wet surfaces will

a affect your stopping distance

b affect your road holding

c make it easy to see unlit objects

d make it hard to see unlit objects

Question 39

Mark one answer

Driving a vehicle fitted with anti-lock brakes allows you to

a brake harder because it is impossible to skid

b drive at higher speeds

c steer and brake at the same time

d pay less attention to the road ahead

Question 40

Mark one answer

You are riding in heavy rain when your rear wheel skids as you accelerate. To get control again you must

a change down to a lower gear

b ease off the throttle

c brake to reduce speed

d put your feet down

Question 41

Mark one answer

When would an anti-lock braking system start to work?

a After the parking brake has been applied

b When ever pressure on the brake pedal is applied

c Just as the wheels are about to lock

d When the normal braking system fails to operate

Question 42

Mark one answer

Anti-lock brakes will take effect when

a you do not brake quickly enough

b excessive brake pressure has been applied

c you have not seen a hazard ahead

d speeding on slippery road surfaces

Question 43

Mark one answer

Anti-lock brakes can greatly assist with

a a higher cruising speed

b steering control when braking

c control when accelerating

d motorway driving

Question 44

Mark one answer

It is snowing. Before starting your journey you should

a think if you need to ride at all

b try to avoid taking a passenger

c plan a route avoiding towns

d take a hot drink before setting out

Question 45

Mark three answers

When driving in fog, which of the following are correct?

a Use dipped headlights

b Use headlights on full beam

c Allow more time for your journey

d Keep close to the car in front

e Slow down

f Use side lights only

Question 46

Mark one answer

Why should you ride with a dipped headlight on in the daytime?

a It helps other road users to see you

b It means that you can ride faster

c Other vehicles will get out of the way

d So that it is already on when it gets dark

Question 47

Mark one answer

You are on a fast, open road in good conditions. For safety, the distance between you and the vehicle in front should be

a a two-second time gap

b one car length

c 2 metres (6 feet 6 inches)

d two car lengths

Question 48

Mark one answer

Motorcyclists are only allowed to use high-intensity rear fog lights when

a a pillion passenger is being carried

b they ride a large touring machine

c visibility is 100 metres (328 feet) or less

d they are riding on the road for the first time

Question 49

Mark one answer

What is the most common cause of skidding?

a Worn tyres

b Driver error

c Other vehicles

d Pedestrians

Question 50

Mark one answer

You are driving in heavy rain. Your steering suddenly becomes very light. You should

a steer towards the side of the road

b apply gentle acceleration

c brake firmly to reduce speed

d ease off the accelerator

Question 51

Mark one answer

Ford

You are driving along a country road. You see this sign. AFTER dealing safely with the hazard you should always

a check your tyre pressures

b switch on your hazard warning lights

c accelerate briskly

d test your brakes

Question 52

Mark one answer

Braking distances on ice can be

a twice the normal distance

b five times the normal distance

c seven times the normal distance

d ten times the normal distance

Question 53

Mark two answers

When riding at night you should

a ride with your headlight on dipped beam

b wear reflective clothing

c wear a tinted visor

d ride in the centre of the road

e give arm signals

Question 54

Mark one answer

Freezing conditions will affect the distance it takes you to come to a stop. You should expect stopping distances to increase by up to

a two times

b three times

c five times

d ten times

Question 55

Mark three answers

You MUST use your headlight

a when riding in a group

b at night when street lighting is poor

c when carrying a passenger

d on motorways during darkness

e at times of poor visibility

f when parked on an unlit road

Question 56

Mark one answer

You are driving on an icy road. How can you avoid wheelspin?

a Drive at a slow speed in as high a gear as possible

b Use the handbrake if the wheels start to slip

c Brake gently and repeatedly

d Drive in a low gear at all times

Question 57

Mark two answers

You are riding through a flood. Which TWO should you do?

a Keep in a high gear and stand up on the footrests

b Keep the engine running fast to keep water out of the exhaust

c Ride slowly and test your brakes when you are out of the water

d Turn your headlight off to avoid any electrical damage

Question 58

Mark one answer

Skidding is mainly caused by

a the weather

b the driver

c the vehicle

d the road

Question 59

Mark one answer

You have just ridden through a flood. When clear of the water you should test your

a starter motor

b headlight

c steering

d brakes

Question 60

Mark two answers

You are driving in freezing conditions. What should you do when approaching a sharp bend?

a Slow down before you reach the bend

b Gently apply your handbrake

c Firmly use your footbrake

d Coast into the bend

e Avoid sudden steering movements

Question 61

Mark one answer

When going through flood water you should ride

a quickly in a high gear

b slowly in a high gear

c quickly in a low gear

d slowly in a low gear

Question 62

Mark one answer

You are turning left on a slippery road. The back of your vehicle slides to the right. You should

a brake firmly and not turn the steering wheel

b steer carefully to the left

c steer carefully to the right

d brake firmly and steer to the left

Question 63

Mark two answers

You have to ride in foggy weather.
You should

a stay close to the centre of the road

b switch only your sidelights on

c switch on your dipped headlights

d be aware of others not using their headlights

e always ride in the gutter to see the kerb

Question 64

Mark one answer

You are braking on a wet road. Your vehicle begins to skid. Your vehicle does not have anti-lock brakes. What is the FIRST thing you should do?

a Quickly pull up the handbrake

b Release the footbrake fully

c Push harder on the brake pedal

d Gently use the accelerator

Question 65

Mark one answer

When riding at night you should NOT

a switch on full beam headlights

b overtake slower vehicles in front

c use dipped beam headlights

d use tinted glasses, lenses or visors

Question 66

Mark one answer

How can you tell when you are driving over black ice?

a It is easier to brake

b The noise from your tyres sounds louder

c You see black ice on the road

d Your steering feels light

Question 67

Mark one answer

At a mini roundabout it is important that a motorcyclist should avoid

a turning right

b using signals

c taking lifesavers

d the painted area

Question 68

Mark one answer

Coasting the vehicle

a improves the driver's control

b makes steering easier

c reduces the driver's control

d uses more fuel

Question 69

Mark two answers

Which of the following should you do when riding in fog?

a Keep close to the vehicle in front

b Use your dipped headlight

c Ride close to the centre of the road

d Keep your visor or goggles clear

e Keep the vehicle in front in view

Question 70

Mark four answers

Before starting a journey in freezing weather you should clear ice and snow from your vehicle's

a aerial

b windows

c bumper

d lights

e mirrors

f number plates

Question 71

Mark two answers

You are riding on a motorway in a crosswind. You should take extra care when

a approaching service areas

b overtaking a large vehicle

c riding in slow-moving traffic

d approaching an exit

e riding in exposed places

Question 72

Mark one answer

You are driving in falling snow. Your wipers are not clearing the windscreen. You should

a set the windscreen demister to cool

b be prepared to clear the windscreen by hand

c use the windscreen washers

d partly open the front windows

Question 73

Mark one answer

You are trying to move off on snow. You should use

a the lowest gear you can

b the highest gear you can

c a high engine speed

d the handbrake and footbrake together

Question 74

Mark one answer

When driving in falling snow you should

a brake firmly and quickly

b be ready to steer sharply

c use sidelights only

d brake gently in plenty of time

Question 75

Mark one answer

The MAIN benefit of having four-wheel drive is to improve

a road holding

b fuel consumption

c stopping distances

d passenger comfort

Question 76

Mark one answer

When driving in fog in daylight you should use

a sidelights

b full beam headlights

c hazard lights

d dipped headlights

Question 77

Mark two answers

In very hot weather the road surface can get soft. Which TWO of the following will be affected most?

a The suspension

b The grip of the tyres

c The braking

d The exhaust

Question 78

Mark one answer

Where are you most likely to be affected by a sidewind?

a On a narrow country lane

b On an open stretch of road

c On a busy stretch of road

d On a long, straight road

Question 79

Mark one answer

In windy conditions you need to take extra care when

a using the brakes

b making a hill start

c turning into a narrow road

d passing pedal cyclists

Question 80

Mark one answer

You are about to go down a steep hill. To control the speed of your vehicle you should

a select a high gear and use the brakes carefully

b select a high gear and use the brakes firmly

c select a low gear and use the brakes carefully

d select a low gear and avoid using the brakes

Question 81

Mark one answer

You are on a long, downhill slope. What should you do to help control the speed of your vehicle?

a Select neutral

b Select a lower gear

c Grip the handbrake firmly

d Apply the parking brake gently

Question 82

Mark one answer

How can you use the engine of your vehicle as a brake?

a By changing to a lower gear

b By selecting reverse gear

c By changing to a higher gear

d By selecting neutral gear

Question 83

Mark two answers

You wish to park facing DOWNHILL. Which TWO of the following should you do?

a Turn the steering wheel towards the kerb

b Park close to the bumper of another car

c Park with two wheels on the kerb

d Put the handbrake on firmly

e Turn the steering wheel away from the kerb

Question 84

Mark one answer

You are driving in a built-up area. You approach a speed hump. You should

a move across to the left-hand side of the road

b wait for any pedestrians to cross

c slow your vehicle right down

d stop and check both pavements

Question 85

Mark one answer

The roads are icy. You should drive slowly

a in the highest gear possible

b in the lowest gear possible

c with the handbrake partly on

d with your left foot on the brake

Question 86

Mark one answer

You are driving along a wet road.
How can you tell if your vehicle is
aquaplaning?

a The engine will stall

b The engine noise will increase

c The steering will feel very heavy

d The steering will feel very light

Question 87

Mark one answer

You have just gone through deep water.
To dry off the brakes you should

a accelerate and keep to a high speed
for a short time

b go slowly while gently applying the
brakes

c avoid using the brakes at all for a
few miles

d stop for at least an hour to allow them
time to dry

Question 88

Mark two answers

How can you tell if you are driving
on ice?

a The tyres make a rumbling noise

b The tyres make hardly any noise

c The steering becomes heavier

d The steering becomes lighter

Answers and explanations

Q001 d	Q024 a
Q002 b	Q025 d
Q003 b	Q026 c You should brake rapidly and firmly.
Q004 d	
Q005 d	Q027 b, c
Q006 a	Q028 c Remember, therefore, to allow a bigger gap when following another vehicle.
Q007 c	
Q008 a	
Q009 b	Q029 b
Q010 b	Q030 b
Q011 b	Q031 c
Q012 a, b	Q032 d
Q013 a	Q033 b A vehicle fitted with anti-lock brakes is very difficult, but not impossible, to skid. Take care if the road surface is loose or wet.
Q014 d Your brakes may be wet. The first thing you should do is check them and then dry them.	
Q015 b, c	Q034 d
Q016 a You can see further round the bend earlier if you keep to the left.	Q035 b, c
	Q036 a, b, d, f
	Q037 c
Q017 a, c, e	Q038 d
Q018 a	Q039 c
Q019 a Note this is the braking distance. The overall stopping distance is further because you have to add 'thinking' distance.	Q040 b
	Q041 c
	Q042 b
	Q043 b
Q020 a, b	Q044 a
Q021 b	Q045 a, c, e
Q022 b	
Q023 b	

Answers and explanations

Q046 a Motorcycles are small and difficult to see. Anything that increases your chances of being seen by other road users is a good thing.

Q047 a

Q048 c

Q049 b

Q050 d This problem is sometimes called aquaplaning. Your tyres build up a thin film of water between them and the road and lose all grip. The steering suddenly feels light and probably uncontrollable. The solution is to ease off the accelerator until you feel the tyres grip the road again.

Q051 d Drive slowly forwards with your left foot gently on the footbrake. This helps dry out the brakes.

Q052 d

Q053 a, b

Q054 d

Q055 b, d, e

Q056 a

Q057 b, c

Q058 b Skidding is usually caused by harsh braking, harsh acceleration or harsh steering – all actions of the driver. You are, however, more likely to cause a skid in a poorly maintained car, in bad weather or on a poor road surface.

Q059 d

Q060 a, e Braking on an icy bend is extremely dangerous. It could cause your vehicle to spin.

Q061 d

Q062 c

Q063 c, d

Q064 b Note that the question asks for the first thing you should do, which is always to remove the cause of the skid – in this case braking. You would next need to re-apply the brakes more gently. 'c' is wrong because braking harder would increase the skid.

Q065 d

Q066 d Black ice is normally invisible when you are driving. The tyres will lose grip with the road which will make the steering feel light.

Answers and explanations

Q067   d

Q068   c Coasting means driving along with the clutch pedal down. This disconnects the engine and gears from the drive wheels of the car, so you have less control.

Q069   b, d

Q070   b, d, e, f

Q071   b, e

Q072   b Bear in mind that you would have to stop first.

Q073   b A higher gear helps avoid wheelspin.

Q074   d

Q075   a

Q076   d Sidelights are not enough so 'a' is wrong. Full beam headlights tend to reflect back the fog, so 'b' is also incorrect.

Q077   b, c

Q078   b

Q079   d In windy conditions cyclists are all too easily blown about and may wobble or steer off course.

Q080   c A low gear will help control your speed, but on a steep hill you will also need your brakes.

Q081   b You should ideally have selected the lower gear before starting down the slope. 'a' would be likely to make your car go faster as you would no longer be in any gear at all.

Q082   a

Q083   a, d If the handbrake should fail, the car will roll into the kerb and not down the road.

Q084   c

Q085   a

Q086   d

Q087   b

Q088   b, d

Theory Test Questions

2001/2002

Hazard Awareness

BSM
We won't fail you

Question 1

Mark <u>one</u> <u>answer</u>

In areas where there are 'traffic calming' measures you should

a drive at a reduced speed

b always drive at the speed limit

c position in the centre of the road

d only slow down if pedestrians are near

Question 2

Mark <u>one</u> <u>answer</u>

You start to feel tired while driving. What should you do?

a Increase your speed slightly

b Decrease your speed slightly

c Find a less busy route

d Pull over at a safe place to rest

Question 3

Mark <u>one</u> <u>answer</u>

You find that you need glasses to read vehicle number plates at the required distance. When MUST you wear them?

a Only in bad weather conditions

b At all times when driving

c Only when you think it necessary

d Only in bad light or at night time

Question 4

Mark <u>three</u> <u>answers</u>

What else can seriously affect your concentration, other than alcoholic drinks?

a Drugs

b Tiredness

c Tinted windows

d Contact lenses

e Loud music

Question 5

Mark <u>one</u> <u>answer</u>

You are planning a long journey. Do you need to plan rest stops?

a Yes, you should plan to stop every half an hour

b Yes, regular stops help concentration

c No, you will be less tired if you get there as soon as possible

d No, only fuel stops will be needed

Question 6

Mark one answer

The red lights are flashing. What should you do when approaching this level crossing?

a Go through quickly

b Go through carefully

c Stop before the barrier

d Switch on hazard warning lights

Question 7

Mark two answers

What are TWO main hazards you should be aware of when going along this street?

a Glare from the sun

b Car doors opening suddenly

c Lack of road markings

d The headlights on parked cars being switched on

e Large goods vehicles

f Children running out from between vehicles

Question 8

Mark one answer

What is the main hazard you should be aware of when following this cyclist?

a The cyclist may move into the left and dismount

b The cyclist may swerve out into the road

c The contents of the cyclist's carrier may fall onto the road

d The cyclist may wish to turn right at the end of the road

Question 9

Mark one answer

You are about to ride home. You cannot find the glasses you need to wear. You should

a ride home slowly, keeping to quiet roads

b borrow a friend's glasses and use those

c ride home at night, so that the lights will help you

d find a way of getting home without riding

Question 10

Mark one answer

You are driving on this dual carriageway. Why may you need to slow down?

a There is a broken white line in the centre

b There are solid white lines either side

c There are roadworks ahead of you

d There are no footpaths

Question 11

Mark three answers

Which THREE result from drinking alcohol?

a Less control

b A false sense of confidence

c Faster reactions

d Poor judgement of speed

e Greater awareness of danger

Question 12

Mark one answer

You have just been overtaken by this motorcyclist who is cutting in sharply. You should

a sound the horn

b brake firmly

c keep a safe gap

d flash your lights

Question 13

Mark three answers

Which THREE of these are likely effects of drinking alcohol?

a Reduced co-ordination

b Increased confidence

c Poor judgement

d Increased concentration

e Faster reactions

f Colour blindness

Question 14

Mark two answers

When approaching this hazard why should you slow down?

a Because of the bend

b Because it's hard to see to the right

c Because of approaching traffic

d Because of animals crossing

e Because of the level crossing

Question 15

Mark one answer

Your doctor has given you a course of medicine. Why should you ask how it will affect you?

a Drugs make you a better rider by quickening your reactions

b You will have to let your insurance company know about the medicine

c Some types of medicine can cause your reactions to slow down

d The medicine you take may affect your hearing

Question 16

Mark one answer

You are about to drive home. You cannot find the glasses you need to wear. You should

a drive home slowly, keeping to quiet roads

b borrow a friend's glasses and use those

c drive home at night, so that the lights will help you

d find a way of getting home without driving

Question 17

Mark two answers

You are not sure if your cough medicine will affect you. What TWO things could you do?

a Ask your doctor

b Check the medicine label

c Ride if you feel alright

d Ask a friend or relative for advice

Question 18

Mark one answer

You find that you need glasses to read vehicle number plates at the required distance. When MUST you wear them?

a Only in bad weather conditions

b At all times when riding

c Only when you think it necessary

d Only in bad light or at night time

Question 19

Mark <u>one</u> answer

How does alcohol affect you?

a It speeds up your reactions

b It increases your awareness

c It improves your co-ordination

d It reduces your concentration

Question 20

Mark <u>three</u> answers

Drinking any amount of alcohol is likely to

a slow down your reactions to hazards

b increase the speed of your reactions

c worsen your judgement of speed

d improve your awareness of danger

e give a false sense of confidence

Question 21

Mark <u>one</u> answer

Your doctor has given you a course of medicine. Why should you ask how it will affect you?

a Drugs make you a better driver by quickening your reactions

b You will have to let your insurance company know about the medicine

c Some types of medicine can cause your reactions to slow down

d The medicine you take may affect your hearing

Question 22

Mark <u>two</u> answers

You are not sure if your cough medicine will affect you. What TWO things could you do?

a Ask your doctor

b Check the medicine label

c Drive if you feel alright

d Ask a friend or relative for advice

Question 23

Mark <u>one</u> answer

Which of the following types of glasses should NOT be worn when riding at night?

a Half-moon

b Round

c Bi-focal

d Tinted

Question 24

Mark <u>one</u> answer

You are on a motorway. You feel tired. You should

a carry on but go slowly

b leave the motorway at the next exit

c complete your journey as quickly as possible

d stop on the hard shoulder

Question 25

Mark one answer

You are about to ride home. You cannot find the glasses you need to wear. You should

a go home slowly, keeping to quiet roads

b borrow a friend's glasses and use those

c go home at night, so that the lights will help you

d find a way of getting home without riding

Question 26

Mark one answer

A driver does something that upsets you. You should

a try not to react

b let them know how you feel

c flash your headlights several times

d sound your horn

Question 27

Mark two answers

Which TWO things would help to keep you alert during a long journey?

a Finishing your journey as fast as you can

b Keeping off the motorways and using country roads

c Making sure that you get plenty of fresh air

d Making regular stops for refreshments

Question 28

Mark one answer

Your doctor has given you a course of medicine. Why should you ask how it will affect you?

a Drugs make you a better rider by quickening your reactions

b You will have to let your insurance company know about the medicine

c Some types of medicine can cause your reactions to slow down

d The medicine you take may affect your hearing

Question 29

Mark one answer

A driver's behaviour has upset you. It may help if you

a stop and take a break

b shout abusive language

c gesture to them with your hand

d follow their car, flashing the headlights

Question 30

Mark one answer

Which of the following types of glasses should NOT be worn when driving at night?

a Half-moon

b Round

c Bi-focal

d Tinted

Question 31

Mark one answer

You see this sign on the rear of a slow-moving lorry that you want to pass.
It is travelling in the middle lane of a three-lane motorway. You should

a cautiously approach the lorry then pass on either side

b follow the lorry until you can leave the motorway

c wait on the hard shoulder until the lorry has stopped

d approach with care and keep to the left of the lorry

Question 32

Mark two answers

Where would you expect to see these markers?

a On a motorway sign

b At the entrance to a narrow bridge

c On a large goods vehicle

d On a builder's skip placed on the road

Question 33

Mark one answer

What does this signal from a police officer mean to oncoming traffic?

a Go ahead

b Stop

c Turn left

d Turn right

Question 34

Mark one answer

What is the main hazard shown in this picture?

a Vehicles turning right

b Vehicles doing U-turns

c The cyclist crossing the road

d Parked cars around the corner

Question 35

Mark one answer

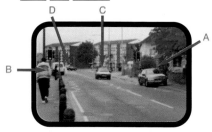

Which road user has caused a hazard?

a The parked car (arrowed A)

b The pedestrian waiting to cross (arrowed B)

c The moving car (arrowed C)

d The car turning (arrowed D)

Question 36

Mark one answer

What should the driver of the car approaching the crossing do?

a Continue at the same speed

b Sound the horn

c Drive through quickly

d Slow down and get ready to stop

Question 37

Mark one answer

What should the driver of the red car do?

a Wave the pedestrians who are waiting to cross

b Wait for the pedestrian in the road to cross

c Quickly drive behind the pedestrian in the road

d Tell the pedestrian in the road she should not have crossed

Question 38

Mark three answers

What THREE things should the driver of the grey car (arrowed) be especially aware of?

a Pedestrians stepping out between cars

b Other cars behind the grey car

c Doors opening on parked cars

d The bumpy road surface

e Cars leaving parking spaces

f Empty parking spaces

Question 39

Mark one answer

What should the driver of the red car (arrowed) do?

a Sound the horn to tell other drivers where he is

b Squeeze through the gap

c Wave the driver of the white car to go on

d Wait until the car blocking the way has moved

Question 40

Mark one answer

What should the driver of the grey car (arrowed) do?

a Cross if the way is clear

b Reverse out of the box junction

c Wait in the same place until the lights are green

d Wait until the lights are red then cross

Question 41

Mark one answer

A

D

C

B

The driver of which car has caused a hazard?

a Car A

b Car B

c Car C

d Car D

Question 42

Mark one answer

You think the driver of the vehicle in front has forgotten to cancel the right indicator. You should

a flash your lights to alert the driver

b sound your horn before overtaking

c overtake on the left if there is room

d stay behind and not overtake

Question 43

Mark one answer

What main hazard should the driver of the red car (arrowed) be most aware of?

a Glare from the sun may affect the driver's vision

b The black car may stop suddenly

c The bus may move out into the road

d Oncoming vehicles will assume the driver is turning right

Question 44

Mark one answer

In heavy motorway traffic you are being followed closely by the vehicle behind. How can you lower the risk of an accident?

a Increase your distance from the vehicle in front

b Tap your foot on the brake pedal sharply

c Switch on your hazard lights

d Move onto the hard shoulder and stop

Question 45

Mark one answer

What does the solid white line at the side of the road indicate?

a Traffic lights ahead

b Edge of the carriageway

c Footpath on the left

d Cycle path

Question 46

Mark one answer

You see this sign ahead. You should expect the road to

a go steeply uphill

b go steeply downhill

c bend sharply to the left

d bend sharply to the right

Question 47

Mark one answer

You are approaching this cyclist.
You should

a overtake before the cyclist gets to the junction

b flash your headlights at the cyclist

c slow down and allow the cyclist to turn

d overtake the cyclist on the left-hand side

Question 48

Mark one answer

Why must you take extra care when turning right at this junction?

a Road surface is poor

b Footpaths are narrow

c Road markings are faint

d There is reduced visibility

Question 49

Mark one answer

This yellow sign on a vehicle indicates this is

a a vehicle broken down

b a school bus

c an ice cream van

d a private ambulance

Question 50

Mark one answer

You are driving towards this level crossing. What would be the first warning of an approaching train?

a Both half barriers down

b A steady amber light

c One half barrier down

d Twin flashing red lights

Question 51

Mark two answers

You get cold and wet when riding.
Which TWO are likely to happen?

a You may lose concentration

b You may slide off the seat

c Your visor may freeze up

d Your reaction times may be slower

e Your helmet may loosen

Question 52

Mark two answers

You are driving along this motorway. It is
raining. When following this lorry you
should

a allow at least a two-second gap

b move left and drive on the hard
shoulder

c allow at least a four-second gap

d be aware of spray reducing your
vision

e move right and stay in the right-hand
lane

Question 53

Mark one answer

You are behind this cyclist. When
the traffic lights change, what should
you do?

a Try to move off before the cyclist

b Allow the cyclist time and room

c Turn right but give the cyclist room

d Tap your horn and drive through first

Question 54

Mark one answer

You are driving towards this left hand
bend. What dangers should you be
aware of?

a A vehicle overtaking you

b No white lines in the centre of
the road

c No sign to warn you of the bend

d Pedestrians walking towards you

Question 55

Mark one answer

Why should you check over your shoulder before turning right into a side road?

a To make sure the road is clear

b To check for emerging traffic

c To check for overtaking vehicles

d To confirm your intention to turn

Question 56

Mark one answer

When approaching this bridge you should give way to

a bicycles

b buses

c motorcycles

d cars

Question 57

Mark one answer

What could happen if you do not keep to the left on right-hand bends?

a You may not be able to see overtaking vehicles

b You may not be able to judge the sharpness of the bend

c Your head may cross over the centre line

d You may not be able to see vehicles to the rear

Question 58

Mark one answer

What type of vehicle could you expect to meet in the middle of the road?

a Lorry

b Bicycle

c Car

d Motorcycle

Question 59

Mark one answer

You are riding up to a zebra crossing. You intend to stop for waiting pedestrians. How could you let them know you are stopping?

a By signalling with your left arm
b By waving them across
c By flashing your headlight
d By signalling with your right arm

Question 60

Mark one answer

While driving, you see this sign ahead. You should

a stop at the sign
b slow, but continue around the bend
c slow to a crawl and continue
d stop and look for open farm gates

Question 61

Mark one answer

Why should the junction on the left be kept clear?

a To allow vehicles to enter and emerge
b To allow the bus to reverse
c To allow vehicles to make a 'U' turn
d To allow vehicles to park

Question 62

Mark one answer

When the traffic lights change to green the white car should

a wait for the cyclist to pull away
b move off quickly and turn in front of the cyclist
c move close up to the cyclist to beat the lights
d sound the horn to warn the cyclist

Question 63

Mark one answer

You intend to turn left at the traffic lights. Just before turning you should

a check your right mirror

b move close up to the white car

c straddle the lanes

d check for bicycles on your left

Question 64

Mark one answer

You should reduce your speed when driving along this road because

a there is a staggered junction ahead

b there is a low bridge ahead

c there is a change in the road surface

d the road ahead narrows

Question 65

Mark one answer

You are driving at 60 mph. As you approach this hazard you should

a maintain your speed

b reduce your speed

c take the next right turn

d take the next left turn

Question 66

Mark two answers

The traffic ahead of you in the left lane is slowing. You should

a be wary of cars on your right cutting in

b accelerate past the vehicles in the left lane

c pull up on the left-hand verge

d move across and continue in the right-hand lane

e slow down keeping a safe separation distance

Question 67

Mark one answer

What might you expect to happen in this situation?

a Traffic will move into the right-hand lane

b Traffic speed will increase

c Traffic will move into the left-hand lane

d Traffic will not need to change position

Question 68

Mark one answer

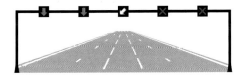

You are driving on a road with several lanes. You see these signs above the lanes. What do they mean?

a The two right lanes are open

b The two left lanes are open

c Traffic in the left lanes should stop

d Traffic in the right lanes should stop

Question 69

Mark one answer

At this blind junction you must stop

a behind the line, then edge forward to see clearly

b beyond the line at a point where you can see clearly

c only if there is traffic on the main road

d only if you are turning to the right

Question 70

Mark two answers

As a provisional licence holder, you must not drive a motor car

a at more than 50 mph

b on your own

c on the motorway

d under the age of 18 years of age at night

e with passengers in the rear seats

Question 71

Mark one answer

As a driver you find that your eyesight has become very poor. Your optician says they cannot help you. The law says that you should tell

a the licensing authority

b your own doctor

c the local police station

d another optician

Question 72

Mark one answer

After passing your driving test, you suffer from ill health. This affects your driving. You MUST

a inform your local police station

b get on as best you can

c not inform anyone as you hold a full licence

d inform the licensing authority

Question 73

Mark one answer

You are invited to a pub lunch. You know that you will have to drive in the evening. What is your best course of action?

a Avoid mixing your alcoholic drinks

b Not drink any alcohol at all

c Have some milk before drinking alcohol

d Eat a hot meal with your alcoholic drinks

Question 74

Mark one answer

You have been convicted of driving while unfit through drink or drugs. You will find this is likely to cause the cost of one of the following to rise considerably. Which one?

a Road fund licence

b Insurance premiums

c Vehicle test certificate

d Driving licence

Question 75

Mark one answer

What advice should you give to a driver who has had a few alcoholic drinks at a party?

a Have a strong cup of coffee and then drive home

b Drive home carefully and slowly

c Go home by public transport

d Wait a short while and then drive home

Question 76

Mark one answer

You go to a social event and need to drive a short time after. What precaution should you take?

a Avoid drinking alcohol on an empty stomach

b Drink plenty of coffee after drinking alcohol

c Avoid drinking alcohol completely

d Drink plenty of milk before drinking alcohol

Question 77

Mark one answer

You have been taking medicine for a few days which made you feel drowsy. Today you feel better but still need to take the medicine. You should only drive

a if your journey is necessary

b at night on quiet roads

c if someone goes with you

d after checking with your doctor

Question 78

Mark one answer

You are about to return home from holiday when you become ill. A doctor prescribes drugs which are likely to affect your driving. You should

a drive only if someone is with you

b avoid driving on motorways

c not drive yourself

d never drive at more than 30 mph

Question 79

Mark two answers

During periods of illness your ability to drive may be impaired. You MUST

a see your doctor each time before you drive

b only take smaller doses of any medicines

c be medically fit to drive

d not drive after taking certain medicines

e take all your medicines with you when you drive

Question 80

Mark one answer

You take some cough medicine given to you by a friend. What should you do before driving?

a Ask your friend if taking the medicine affected their driving

b Drink some strong coffee one hour before driving

c Check the label to see if the medicine will affect your driving

d Drive a short distance to see if the medicine is affecting your driving

Question 81

Mark two answers

You feel drowsy when driving. You should

a stop and rest as soon as possible

b turn the heater up to keep you warm and comfortable

c make sure you have a good supply of fresh air

d continue with your journey but drive more slowly

e close the car windows to help you concentrate

Question 82

Mark <u>two</u> <u>answers</u>

You are driving along a motorway and become tired. You should

a stop at the next service area and rest

b leave the motorway at the next exit and rest

c increase your speed and turn up the radio volume

d close all your windows and set heating to warm

e pull up on the hard shoulder and change drivers

Question 83

Mark <u>one</u> <u>answer</u>

You are taking drugs that are likely to affect your driving. What should you do?

a Seek medical advice before driving

b Limit your driving to essential journeys

c Only drive if accompanied by a full licence-holder

d Drive only for short distances

Question 84

Mark <u>one</u> <u>answer</u>

You are about to drive home. You feel very tired and have a severe headache. You should

a wait until you are fit and well before driving

b drive home, but take a tablet for headaches

c drive home if you can stay awake for the journey

d wait for a short time, then drive home slowly

Question 85

Mark <u>one</u> <u>answer</u>

If you are feeling tired it is best to stop as soon as you can. Until then you should

a increase your speed to find a stopping place quickly

b ensure a supply of fresh air

c gently tap the steering wheel

d keep changing speed to improve concentration

Question 86

Mark one answer

If your motorway journey seems boring and you feel drowsy whilst driving you should

a open a window and drive to the next service area

b stop on the hard shoulder for a sleep

c speed up to arrive at your destination sooner

d slow down and let other drivers overtake

Question 87

Mark three answers

Driving long distances can be tiring. You can prevent this by

a stopping every so often for a walk

b opening a window for some fresh air

c ensuring plenty of refreshment breaks

d completing the journey without stopping

e eating a large meal before driving

Question 88

Mark three answers

Which THREE are likely to make you lose concentration while driving?

a Looking at road maps

b Listening to loud music

c Using your windscreen washers

d Looking in your wing mirror

e Using a mobile phone

Question 89

Mark one answer

A driver pulls out of a side road in front of you. You have to brake hard. You should

a ignore the error and stay calm

b flash your lights to show your annoyance

c sound your horn to show your annoyance

d overtake as soon as possible

Question 90

Mark one answer

An elderly person's driving ability could be affected because they may be unable to

a obtain car insurance

b understand road signs

c react very quickly

d give signals correctly

Question 91

Mark one answer

You take the wrong route and find you are on a one-way street. You should

a reverse out of the road

b turn round in a side road

c continue to the end of the road

d reverse into a driveway

Question 92

Mark one answer

You have just passed these warning lights. What hazard would you expect to see next?

a A level crossing with no barrier

b An ambulance station

c A school crossing patrol

d An opening bridge

Question 93

Mark one answer

You are driving along this road. The driver on the left is reversing from a driveway. You should

a move to the opposite side of the road

b drive through as you have priority

c sound your horn and be prepared to stop

d speed up and drive through quickly

Question 94

Mark two answers

Why should you be especially cautious when going past this bus?

a There is traffic approaching in the distance

b The driver may open the door

c It may suddenly move off

d People may cross the road in front of it

e There are bicycles parked on the pavement

Question 95

Mark one answer

You have been involved in an argument before starting your journey. This has made you feel angry. You should

a start to drive, but open a window

b drive slower than normal and turn your radio on

c have an alcoholic drink to help you relax before driving

d calm down before you start to drive

Answers and explanations

Q001 a Road humps and rumble strips are examples of traffic calming measures. They are often found in residential areas and have been introduced to reduce the overall speed of traffic.

Q002 d A short nap of 10 to 15 minutes is the most effective way of feeling refreshed if you start to feel tired when driving. Many accidents happen because people fall asleep at the wheel.

Q003 b If you need glasses to drive you must wear them whenever you are driving, so 'b' is correct.

Q004 a, b, e

Q005 b

Q006 c

Q007 b, f

Q008 b

Q009 d It is illegal to ride a motorcycle if you cannot satisfy the requirements of the eyesight test.

Q010 c

Q011 a, b, d

Q012 c

Q013 a, b, c

Q014 a, e

Q015 c

Q016 d

Q017 a, b

Q018 b

Q019 d You may well feel, after drinking, that 'a', 'b' and 'c' are true. However, this is never correct and makes you dangerous.

Q020 a, c, e

Q021 c

Q022 a, b

Q023 d

Q024 b If you feel tired you greatly increase your chances of having an accident. You must stop, but as you are on a motorway you cannot do this unless you leave at the next exit or find a service station before it.

Q025 d

Q026 a

Q027 c, d

Q028 c

Q029 a

Q030 d

Q031 d

Q032 c, d

Q033 b

Answers and explanations

Q034	c
Q035	a
Q036	d
Q037	b
Q038	a, c, e
Q039	d
Q040	a
Q041	a
Q042	d
Q043	c
Q044	a
Q045	b
Q046	c
Q047	c
Q048	d
Q049	b
Q050	b
Q051	a, d
Q052	c, d
Q053	b
Q054	d
Q055	c Overtaking vehicles might not be visible in your mirrors.
Q056	b
Q057	c As you bank over, your head might cross over to the other side of the road if you are too close to the centre line.
Q058	a
Q059	d
Q060	b

Q061	a
Q062	a
Q063	d
Q064	a
Q065	b
Q066	a, e
Q067	c
Q068	b
Q069	a
Q070	b, c
Q071	a You must not drive if your eyesight becomes so poor that you can no longer meet the minimum legal requirements, wearing glasses or contact lenses if necessary.
Q072	d In the event of a short-term illness, like flu, that affected your ability to drive, you would simply not drive until you are recovered.
Q073	b
Q074	b
Q075	c The only sensible answer is don't drink and drive.
Q076	c
Q077	d
Q078	c
Q079	c, d
Q080	c
Q081	a, c

Answers and explanations

Q082   a, b

Q083   a A significant number of drugs,
           even those you can buy in the
           chemist, can affect your ability
           to drive. Sometimes a warning
           is given on the packet, but if in
           any doubt seek medical
           advice.

Q084   a

Q085   b

Q086   a

Q087   a, b, c

Q088   a, b, e

           'c' and 'd' are normal parts of
           the driving task.

Q089   a

Q090   c

Q091   c

Q092   c

Q093   c

Q094   c, d

Q095   d

Theory Test Questions

2001/2002

Vulnerable Road Users

BSM
We won't fail you

Question 1

Mark one answer

SCHOOL KEEP CLEAR

These road markings must be kept clear to allow

a school children to be dropped off

b for teachers to park

c school children to be picked up

d a clear view of the crossing area

Question 2

Mark one answer

SCHOOL KEEP CLEAR

You must not stop on these road markings because you may obstruct

a children's view of the crossing area

b teachers' access to the school

c delivery vehicles' access to the school

d emergency vehicles' access to the school

Question 3

Mark one answer

The left-hand pavement is closed due to street repairs. What should you do?

a Watch out for pedestrians walking in the road

b Use your right-hand mirror more often

c Speed up to get past the road works quicker

d Position close to the left-hand kerb

Question 4

Mark one answer

SCHOOL KEEP CLEAR

Stopping on these road markings may obstruct

a emergency vehicles' access to the school

b drivers' view of the crossing area

c teachers' access to the school

d delivery vehicles' access to the school

Question 5

Mark one answer

M-SCHOOL KEEP CLEAR-M

Yellow zig zag lines on the road outside schools mean

a sound your horn to alert other road users

b stop to allow children to cross

c you must not wait or park on these lines

d you must not drive over these lines

Question 7

Mark one answer

M-SCHOOL KEEP CLEAR-M

What do these road markings outside a school mean?

a You may park here if you are a teacher

b Sound your horn before parking

c When parking use your hazard warning lights

d You must not wait or park your vehicle here

Question 6

Mark one answer

You are riding in foot flowing traffic. The vehicle behind is following too closely. You should

a slow down gradually to increase the gap in front of you

b slow down as quickly as possible by braking

c accelerate to get away from the vehicle behind you

d apply the brakes sharply to warn the driver behind

Question 8

Mark two answers

You are about to overtake horse riders. Which TWO of the following could scare the horses?

a Sounding your horn

b Giving arm signals

c Riding slowly

d Revving your engine

Question 9

Mark one answer

Where would you see this sign?

a Near a school crossing

b At a playground entrance

c On a school bus

d At a 'pedestrians only' area

Question 10

Mark one answer

You are following a motorcyclist on an uneven road. You should

a allow less room so you can be seen in their mirrors

b overtake immediately

c allow extra room in case they swerve to avoid pot-holes

d allow the same room as normal because road surfaces do not affect motorcyclists

Question 11

Mark one answer

You are following two cyclists. They approach a roundabout in the left-hand lane. In which direction should you expect the cyclists to go?

a Left

b Right

c Any direction

d Straight ahead

Question 12

Mark one answer

You are travelling behind a moped. You want to turn left just ahead. You should

a overtake the moped before the junction

b pull alongside the moped and stay level until just before the junction

c sound your horn as a warning and pull in front of the moped

d stay behind until the moped has passed the junction

Question 13

Mark three answers

Which THREE of the following are hazards motorcyclists present in queues of traffic?

a Cutting in just in front of you

b Riding in single file

c Passing very close to you

d Riding with their headlight on dipped beam

e Filtering between the lanes

Question 14

Mark one answer

You see a horse rider as you approach a roundabout. They are signalling right but keeping well to the left. You should

a proceed as normal

b keep close to them

c cut in front of them

d stay well back

Question 15

Mark one answer

How would you react to drivers who appear to be inexperienced?

a Sound your horn to warn them of your presence

b Be patient and prepare for them to react more slowly

c Flash your headlights to indicate that it is safe for them to proceed

d Overtake them as soon as possible

Question 16

Mark one answer

You are following a learner driver who stalls at a junction. You should

a be patient as you expect them to make mistakes

b stay very close behind and flash your headlights

c start to rev your engine if they take too long to restart

d immediately steer around them and drive on

Question 17

Mark one answer

You are following a car driven by an elderly driver. You should

a expect the driver to drive badly

b flash your lights and overtake

c be aware that the driver's reactions may not be as fast as yours

d stay very close behind but be careful

Question 18

Mark one answer

You are following a cyclist. You wish to turn left just ahead. You should

a overtake the cyclist before the junction

b pull alongside the cyclist and stay level until after the junction

c hold back until the cyclist has passed the junction

d go around the cyclist on the junction

Question 19

Mark one answer

You are driving on a main road. You intend to turn right into a side road. Just before turning you should

a adjust your interior mirror

b flash your headlamps

c steer over to the left

d check for traffic overtaking on your right

Question 20

Mark one answer

A horse rider is in the left-hand lane approaching a roundabout. You should expect the rider to

a go in any direction

b turn right

c turn left

d go ahead

Question 21

Mark one answer

You have just passed your test. How can you decrease your risk of accidents on the motorway?

a By keeping up with the car in front

b By never going over 40 mph

c By staying only in the left-hand lane

d By taking further training

Question 22

Mark one answer

You are on a country road. What should you expect to see coming towards you on YOUR side of the road?

a Motorcycles

b Bicycles

c Pedestrians

d Horse riders

Question 23

Mark <u>one</u> <u>answer</u>

You are turning left into a side road. Pedestrians are crossing the road near the junction. You must

a wave them on

b sound your horn

c switch on your hazard lights

d wait for them to cross

Question 24

Mark <u>one</u> <u>answer</u>

You are riding towards a zebra crossing. Waiting to cross is a person in a wheelchair. You should

a continue on your way

b wave to the person to cross

c wave to the person to wait

d be prepared to stop

Question 25

Mark <u>one</u> <u>answer</u>

Which age group of drivers is most likely to be involved in a road accident?

a 36- to 45-year-olds

b 55-year-olds and over

c 46- to 55-year-olds

d 17- to 25-year-olds

Question 26

Mark <u>one</u> <u>answer</u>

Why should you allow extra room when overtaking another motorcyclist on a windy day?

a The rider may turn off suddenly to get out of the wind

b The rider may be blown across in front of you

c The rider may stop suddenly

d The rider may be travelling faster than normal

Question 27

Mark <u>one</u> <u>answer</u>

The road outside this school is marked with yellow zig zag lines. What do these lines mean?

a You may park on the lines when dropping off school children

b You may park on the lines when picking up school children

c You must not wait or park your vehicle here at all

d You must stay with your vehicle if you park here

Question 28

Mark one answer

The road outside this school is marked with yellow zig zag lines. What do these lines mean?

a You may park on the lines when dropping off school children

b You may park on the lines when picking up school children

c You must not wait or park your motorcycle here at all

d You must stay with your motorcycle if you park here

Question 29

Mark one answer

You are driving towards a zebra crossing. Waiting to cross is a person in a wheelchair. You should

a continue on your way

b wave to the person to cross

c wave to the person to wait

d be prepared to stop

Question 30

Mark two answers

You have stopped at a pelican crossing. A disabled person is crossing slowly in front of you. The lights have now changed to green. You should

a allow the person to cross

b ride in front of the person

c ride behind the person

d sound your horn

e be patient

f edge forward slowly

Question 31

Mark one answer

Where in particular should you look out for motorcyclists?

a In a filling station

b At a road junction

c Near a service area

d When entering a car park

Question 32

Mark one answer

Where should you take particular care to look out for motorcyclists and cyclists?

a On dual carriageways

b At junctions

c At zebra crossings

d On one-way streets

Question 33

Mark one answer

You should not ride too closely behind a lorry because

a you will breathe in the lorry's exhaust fumes

b wind from the lorry will slow you down

c drivers behind you may not be able to see you

d it will reduce your view ahead

Question 34

Mark one answer

Which sign means that there may be people walking along the road?

a　　**b**　　**c**　　**d**

Question 35

Mark one answer

You are riding along a main road with many side roads. Why should you be particularly careful?

a Gusts of wind from the side roads may push you off course

b Drivers coming out from side roads may not see you

c The road will be more slippery where cars have been turning

d Drivers will be travelling slowly when they approach a junction

Question 36

Mark one answer

You are turning left at a junction. Pedestrians have started to cross the road. You should

a go on, giving them plenty of room

b stop and wave at them to cross

c blow your horn and proceed

d give way to them

Question 37

Mark one answer

You are turning left from a main road into a side road. People are already crossing the road into which you are turning. You should

a continue, as it is your right of way

b signal to them to continue crossing

c wait and allow them to cross

d sound your horn to warn them of your presence

Question 38

Mark one answer

You are at a road junction, turning into a minor road. There are pedestrians crossing the minor road. You should

a stop and wave the pedestrians across

b sound your horn to let the pedestrians know that you are there

c give way to the pedestrians who are already crossing

d carry on; the pedestrians should give way to you

Question 39

Mark one answer

You are turning left into a side road. What hazards should you be especially aware of?

a One-way street

b Pedestrians

c Traffic congestion

d Parked vehicles

Question 40

Mark one answer

You want to reverse into a side road. You are not sure that the area behind your car is clear. What should you do?

a Look through the rear window only

b Get out and check

c Check the mirrors only

d Carry on, assuming it is clear

Question 41

Mark one answer

You are about to reverse into a side road. A pedestrian wishes to cross behind you. You should

a wave to the pedestrian to stop

b give way to the pedestrian

c wave to the pedestrian to cross

d reverse before the pedestrian starts to cross

Question 42

Mark one answer

Who is especially in danger of not being seen as you reverse your car?

a Motorcyclists

b Car drivers

c Cyclists

d Children

Question 43

Mark one answer

You are reversing around a corner when you notice a pedestrian walking behind you. What should you do?

a Slow down and wave the pedestrian across

b Continue reversing and steer round the pedestrian

c Stop and give way

d Continue reversing and sound your horn

Question 44

Mark one answer

You intend to turn right into a side road. Just before turning you should check for motorcyclists who might be

a overtaking on your left

b following you closely

c emerging from the side road

d overtaking on your right

Question 45

Mark one answer

You are at the front of a queue of traffic waiting to turn right into a side road. Why is it important to check your right mirror just before turning?

a To look for pedestrians about to cross

b To check for overtaking vehicles

c To make sure the side road is clear

d To check for emerging traffic

Question 46

Mark one answer

You want to turn right from a junction but your view is restricted by parked vehicles. What should you do?

a Move out quickly, but be prepared to stop

b Sound your horn and pull out if there is no reply

c Stop, then move slowly forward until you have a clear view

d Stop, get out and look along the main road to check

Question 47

Mark three answers

In which THREE places would parking your vehicle cause danger or obstruction to other road users?

a In front of a property entrance

b At or near a bus stop

c On your driveway

d In a marked parking space

e On the approach to a level crossing

Question 48

Mark three answers

In which THREE places would parking cause an obstruction to others?

a Near the brow of a hill
b In a lay-by
c Where the kerb is raised
d Where the kerb has been lowered for wheelchairs
e At or near a bus stop

Question 49

Mark one answer

What must a driver do at a pelican crossing when the amber light is flashing?

a Signal the pedestrian to cross
b Always wait for the green light before proceeding
c Give way to any pedestrians on the crossing
d Wait for the red-and-amber light before proceeding

Question 50

Mark two answers

You have stopped at a pelican crossing. A disabled person is crossing slowly in front of you. The lights have now changed to green. You should

a allow the person to cross
b drive in front of the person
c drive behind the person
d sound your horn
e be patient
f edge forward slowly

Question 51

Mark one answer

As you approach a pelican crossing the lights change to green. Elderly people are halfway across. You should

a wave them to cross as quickly as they can
b rev your engine to make them hurry
c flash your lights in case they have not heard you
d wait because they will take longer to cross

Question 52

Mark one answer

A toucan crossing is different from other crossings because

a moped riders can use it
b it is controlled by a traffic warden
c it is controlled by two flashing lights
d cyclists can use it

Question 53

Mark two answers

At toucan crossings

a there is no flashing amber light

b cyclists are not permitted

c there is a continuously flashing amber beacon

d pedestrians and cyclists may cross

e you only stop if someone is waiting to cross

Question 54

Mark one answer

You are driving past parked cars. You notice a wheel of a bicycle sticking out between them. What should you do?

a Accelerate past quickly and sound your horn

b Slow down and wave the cyclist across

c Brake sharply and flash your headlights

d Slow down and be prepared to stop for a cyclist

Question 55

Mark one answer

You are driving past a line of parked cars. You notice a ball bouncing out into the road ahead. What should you do?

a Continue driving at the same speed and sound your horn

b Continue driving at the same speed and flash your headlights

c Slow down and be prepared to stop for children

d Stop and wave the children across to fetch their ball

Question 56

Mark one answer

What does this sign tell you?

a No cycling

b Cycle route ahead

c Route for cycles only

d End of cycle route

Question 57

Mark one answer

How will a school crossing patrol signal you to stop?

a By pointing to children on the opposite pavement

b By displaying a red light

c By displaying a stop sign

d By giving you an arm signal

Question 58

Mark one answer

Where would you see this sign?

a In the window of a car taking children to school

b At the side of the road

c At playground areas

d On the rear of a school bus or coach

Question 59

Mark one answer

Which sign tells you that pedestrians may be walking in the road as there is no pavement?

a   **b**   **c**   **d**

Question 60

Mark one answer

What does this sign mean?

a No route for pedestrians and cyclists

b A route for pedestrians only

c A route for cyclists only

d A route for pedestrians and cyclists

Question 61

Mark one answer

You see a pedestrian with a white stick and red band. This means that the person is

a physically disabled

b deaf only

c blind only

d deaf and blind

Question 62

Mark one answer

What action would you take when elderly people are crossing the road?

a Wave them across so they know that you have seen them

b Be patient and allow them to cross in their own time

c Rev the engine to let them know that you are waiting

d Tap the horn in case they are hard of hearing

Question 63

Mark one answer

You see two elderly pedestrians about to cross the road ahead. You should

a expect them to wait for you to pass

b speed up to get past them quickly

c stop and wave them across the road

d be careful, they may misjudge your speed

Question 64

Mark one answer

What does this sign mean?

a Contra-flow pedal cycle lane

b With-flow pedal cycle lane

c Pedal cycles and buses only

d No pedal cycles or buses

Question 65

Mark one answer

You should NEVER attempt to overtake a cyclist

a just before you turn left

b just before you turn right

c on a one-way street

d on a dual carriageway

Question 66

Mark one answer

You are coming up to a roundabout. A cyclist is signalling to turn right. What should you do?

a Overtake on the right

b Give a horn warning

c Signal the cyclist to move across

d Give the cyclist plenty of room

Question 67

Mark one answer

You are approaching this roundabout and see the cyclist signal right. Why is the cyclist keeping to the left?

a It is a quicker route for the cyclist

b The cyclist is going to turn left instead

c The cyclist thinks The Highway Code does not apply to bicycles

d The cyclist is slower and more vulnerable

Question 68

Mark one answer

When you are overtaking a cyclist you should leave as much room as you would give to a car. What is the main reason for this?

a The cyclist might change lanes

b The cyclist might get off the bike

c The cyclist might swerve

d The cyclist might have to make a right turn

Question 69

Mark two answers

Which TWO should you allow extra room when overtaking?

a Motorcycles

b Tractors

c Bicycles

d Road-sweeping vehicles

Question 70

Mark three answers

You are riding on a country lane. You see cattle on the road. You should

a slow down

b stop if necessary

c give plenty of room

d rev your engine

e sound your horn

f ride up close behind them

Question 71

Mark one answer

Why should you allow extra room when overtaking a motorcyclist on a windy day?

a The rider may turn off suddenly to get out of the wind

b The rider may be blown across in front of you

c The rider may stop suddenly

d The rider may be travelling faster than normal

Question 72

Mark one answer

Why should you look particularly for motorcyclists and cyclists at junctions?

a They may want to turn into the side road

b They may slow down to let you turn

c They are harder to see

d They might not see you turn

Question 73

Mark one answer

You are waiting to come out of a side road. Why should you watch carefully for motorcycles?

a Motorcycles are usually faster than cars

b Police patrols often use motorcycles

c Motorcycles are small and hard to see

d Motorcycles have right of way

Question 74

Mark one answer

In daylight, an approaching motorcyclist is using a dipped headlight. Why?

a So that the rider can be seen more easily

b To stop the battery overcharging

c To improve the rider's vision

d The rider is inviting you to proceed

Question 75

Mark one answer

Riders are more likely to have a serious accident if they

a wear glasses or contact lenses

b have recently passed their test

c are carrying pillion passengers

d have not taken a theory test

Question 76

Mark one answer

Motorcyclists should wear bright clothing mainly because

a they must do so by law

b it helps keep them cool in summer

c the colours are popular

d drivers often do not see them

Question 77

Mark one answer

A learner driver has begun to emerge into your path from a side road on the left. You should

a be ready to slow down and stop

b let them emerge then ride close behind

c turn into the side road

d brake hard, then wave them out

Question 78

Mark one answer

There is a slow-moving motorcyclist ahead of you. You are unsure what the rider is going to do. You should

a pass on the left

b pass on the right

c stay behind

d move closer

Question 79

Mark one answer

The vehicle ahead is being driven by a learner. You should

a keep calm and be patient

b ride up close behind

c put your headlight on full beam

d sound your horn and overtake

Question 80

Mark one answer

Motorcyclists will often look round over their right shoulder just before turning right. This is because

a they need to listen for following traffic

b motorcycles do not have mirrors

c looking around helps them balance as they turn

d they need to check for traffic in their blind area

Question 81

Mark three answers

At road junctions which of the following are most vulnerable?

a Cyclists

b Motorcyclists

c Pedestrians

d Car drivers

e Lorry drivers

Question 82

Mark one answer

You want to turn right from a main road into a side road. Just before turning you should

a cancel your right-turn signal

b select first gear

c check for traffic overtaking on your right

d stop and set the handbrake

Question 83

Mark one answer

Why is it vital for a rider to make a lifesaver check before turning right?

a To check for any overtaking traffic

b To confirm that they are about to turn

c To make sure the side road is clear

d To check that the rear indicator is flashing

Question 84

Mark one answer

Motorcyclists are particularly vulnerable

a when moving off

b on dual carriageways

c when approaching junctions

d on motorways

Question 85

Mark one answer

Ahead of you there is a vehicle with a flashing amber beacon. This means it is

a slow moving

b broken down

c a doctor's car

d a school crossing patrol

Question 86

Mark one answer

You are driving in slow-moving queues of traffic. Just before changing lane you should

a sound the horn

b look for motorcyclists filtering through the traffic

c give a 'slowing down' arm signal

d change down to first gear

Question 87

Mark one answer

An injured motorcyclist is lying unconscious in the road. You should

a remove the safety helmet

b seek medical assistance

c move the person off the road

d remove the leather jacket

Question 88

Mark one answer

You are driving in town. There is a bus at the bus stop on the other side of the road. Why should you be careful?

a The bus may have broken down

b Pedestrians may come from behind the bus

c The bus may move off suddenly

d The bus may romain stationary

Question 89

Mark one answer

How should you overtake horse riders?

a Drive up close and overtake as soon as possible

b Speed is not important but allow plenty of room

c Use your horn just once to warn them

d Drive slowly and leave plenty of room

Question 90

Mark <u>one</u> <u>answer</u>

You notice horse riders in front. What should you do FIRST?

a Pull out to the middle of the road

b Be prepared to slow down

c Accelerate around them

d Signal right

Question 91

Mark <u>two</u> <u>answers</u>

You are approaching a roundabout. There are horses just ahead of you. You should

a be prepared to stop

b treat them like any other vehicle

c give them plenty of room

d accelerate past as quickly as possible

e sound your horn as a warning

Question 92

Mark <u>three</u> <u>answers</u>

Which THREE should you do when passing sheep on a road?

a Allow plenty of room

b Go very slowly

c Pass quickly but quietly

d Be ready to stop

e Briefly sound your horn

Question 93

Mark <u>one</u> <u>answer</u>

You have a collision whilst your car is moving. What is the first thing you must do?

a Stop only if there are injured people

b Call the emergency services

c Stop at the scene of the accident

d Call your insurance company

Question 94

Mark <u>one</u> <u>answer</u>

A friend wants to teach you to drive a car. They must

a be over 21 and have held a full licence for at least two years

b be over 18 and hold an advanced driver's certificate

c be over 18 and have fully comprehensive insurance

d be over 21 and have held a full licence for at least three years

Question 95

Mark one answer

At night you see a pedestrian wearing reflective clothing and carrying a bright red light. What does this mean?

a You are approaching roadworks

b You are approaching an organised walk

c You are approaching a slow-moving vehicle

d You are approaching an accident black spot

Question 96

Mark one answer

You are dazzled at night by a vehicle behind you. You should

a set your mirror to anti dazzle

b set your mirror to dazzle the other driver

c brake sharply to a stop

d switch your rear lights on and off

Question 97

Mark one answer

There are flashing amber lights under a school warning sign. What action should you take?

a Reduce speed until you are clear of the area

b Keep up your speed and sound the horn

c Increase your speed to clear the area quickly

d Wait at the lights until they change to green

Question 98

Mark one answer

Which of the following types of crossing can detect when people are on them?

a Pelican

b Toucan

c Zebra

d Puffin

Question 99

Mark one answer

You are approaching this crossing. You should

a prepare to slow down and stop

b stop and wave the pedestrians across

c speed up and pass by quickly

d drive on unless the pedestrians step out

Question 100

Mark one answer

You see a pedestrian with a dog. The dog has a bright orange lead and collar. This especially warns you that the pedestrian is

a elderly

b dog training

c colour blind

d deaf

Answers and explanations

Q001　d You must not park on these yellow zig zag lines, not even to drop off or pick up children.

Q002　a

Q003　a Remember that pedestrians walking in the road will have their backs to you, so give them plenty of space.

Q004　b

Q005　c

Q006　a

Q007　d

Q008　a, d

Q009　c

Q010　c

Q011　c

Q012　d

Q013　a, c, e
　　　　Check your door mirrors, especially before moving forwards or changing lanes.

Q014　d

Q015　b

Q016　a

Q017　c

Q018　c As the question states you are turning left JUST ahead, you have no time to overtake the cyclist safely which is why 'c' is correct.

Q019　d

Q020　a

Q021　d

Q022　c Pedestrians are the most likely to expect as country roads often have no pavements and pedestrians are advised to walk on the right so that they can see oncoming traffic on their side of the road. However, you should always expect the unexpected when driving.

Q023　d When you turn into a side road pedestrians who are already crossing have priority so you must give way.

Q024　d

Q025　d

Q026　b

Q027　c

Q028　c

Q029　d

Q030　a, e

Q031　b

Q032　b

Q033　d

Q034　d Red triangles give warnings, in this case of people walking along the road. 'c' is a warning of a pedestrian crossing.

Q035　b

Answers and explanations

Q036 d
Q037 c
Q038 c
Q039 b
Q040 b
Q041 b
Q042 d Children are small and you
       may not be able to see them
       through your rear windscreen.
Q043 c
Q044 d
Q045 b
Q046 c You cannot turn right until
       you can see it is safe to do so.
       You should stop and then edge
       slowly forwards until you can
       see clearly to the left and right.
Q047 a, b, e
Q048 a, d, e
Q049 c
Q050 a, e
Q051 d
Q052 d
Q053 a, d
Q054 d
Q055 c
Q056 b
Q057 c
Q058 d
Q059 a
Q060 d

Q061 d
Q062 b
Q063 d The ability to judge speed
       tends to deteriorate as you get
       older.
Q064 b
Q065 a The word 'NEVER' makes
       'a' correct.
Q066 d
Q067 d
Q068 c 'c' is the answer required, but
       you should also be aware that
       cyclists can be unpredictable.
Q069 a, c
       Motorcycles and bicycles can
       easily swerve and you need to
       allow them extra room.
Q070 a, b, c
Q071 b
Q072 c
Q073 c
Q074 a
Q075 b
Q076 d
Q077 a
Q078 c
Q079 a
Q080 d
Q081 a, b, c
Q082 c Use your right-door mirror and
       look particularly for motorcyclists.

Answers and explanations

Q083 a

Q084 c

Q085 a

Q086 b

Q087 b

Q088 b

Q089 d

Q090 b Horses and their riders can be
        unpredictable so 'b' is the
        safest first action.

Q091 a, c

Q092 a, b, d

Q093 c

Q094 d

Q095 b

Q096 a

Q097 a

Q098 d

Q099 a

Q100 d

Theory
Test
Questions

2001/2002

Other Types of Vehicle

BSM
We won't fail you

Question 1

Mark one answer

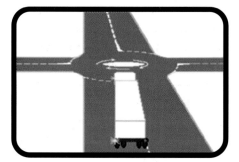

You are following a large articulated vehicle. It is going to turn left into a narrow road. What action should you take?

a Move out and overtake on the right

b Pass on the left as the vehicle moves out

c Be prepared to stop behind

d Overtake quickly before the lorry moves out

Question 2

Mark one answer

You keep well back while waiting to overtake a large vehicle. A car fills the gap. You should

a sound your horn

b drop back further

c flash your headlights

d start to overtake

Question 3

Mark one answer

You are on a wet motorway with surface spray. You should use

a hazard flashers

b dipped headlights

c rear fog lights

d sidelights

Question 4

Mark one answer

The road is wet. Why might a motorcyclist steer round drain covers on a bend?

a To avoid puncturing the tyres on the edge of the drain covers

b To prevent the motorcycle sliding on the metal drain covers

c To help judge the bend using the drain covers as marker points

d To avoid splashing pedestrians on the pavement

Question 5

Mark one answer

It is very windy. You are behind a motorcyclist who is overtaking a high-sided vehicle. What should you do?

a Overtake the motorcyclist immediately

b Keep well back

c Stay level with the motorcyclist

d Keep close to the motorcyclist

Question 6

Mark one answer

It is very windy. You are about to overtake a motorcyclist. You should

a overtake slowly

b allow extra room

c sound your horn

d keep close as you pass

Question 7

Mark one answer

You are about to overtake a slow-moving motorcyclist. Which one of these signs would make you take special care?

   a   **b**   **c**   **d**

Question 8

Mark one answer

You are riding behind a long vehicle. There is a mini-roundabout ahead. The vehicle is signalling left, but positioned to the right. You should

a sound your horn

b overtake on the left

c keep well back

d flash your headlights

Question 9

Mark one answer

You are waiting to emerge left from a minor road. A large vehicle is approaching from the right. You have time to turn, but you should wait. Why?

a The large vehicle can easily hide an overtaking vehicle

b The large vehicle can turn suddenly

c The large vehicle is difficult to steer in a straight line

d The large vehicle can easily hide vehicles from the left

Question 10

Mark one answer

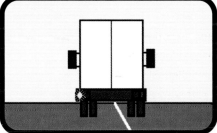

You are following a long vehicle. It approaches a crossroads and signals left, but moves out to the right. You should

a get closer in order to pass it quickly

b stay well back and give it room

c assume the signal is wrong and it is really turning right

d overtake as it starts to slow down

Question 11

Mark <u>one</u> answer

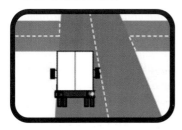

You are following a long vehicle approaching a crossroads. The driver signals right but moves close to the left-hand kerb. What should you do?

a Warn the driver of the wrong signal

b Wait behind the long vehicle

c Report the driver to the police

d Overtake on the right-hand side

Question 12

Mark <u>one</u> answer

You are approaching a mini-roundabout. The long vehicle in front is signalling left but positioned over to the right.
You should

a sound your horn

b overtake on the left

c follow the same course as the lorry

d keep well back

Question 13

Mark <u>one</u> answer
You are towing a caravan. Which is the safest type of rear-view mirror to use?

a Interior wide-angle-view mirror

b Extended-arm side mirrors

c Ordinary door mirrors

d Ordinary interior mirror

Question 14

Mark <u>one</u> answer
Before overtaking a large vehicle you should keep well back. Why is this?

a To give acceleration space to overtake quickly on blind bends

b To get the best view of the road ahead

c To leave a gap in case the vehicle stops and rolls back

d To offer other drivers a safe gap if they want to overtake you

Question 15

Mark <u>one</u> answer
You wish to overtake a long, slow-moving vehicle on a busy road.
You should

a follow it closely and keep moving out to see the road ahead

b flash your headlights for the oncoming traffic to give way

c stay behind until the driver waves you past

d keep well back until you can see that it is clear

Question 16

Mark one answer

You are driving downhill. There is a car parked on the other side of the road. Large, slow lorries are coming towards you. You should

a keep going because you have the right of way

b slow down and give way

c speed up and get past quickly

d pull over on the right behind the parked car

Question 17

Mark one answer

Why is passing a lorry more risky than passing a car?

a Lorries are longer than cars

b Lorries may suddenly pull up

c The brakes of lorries are not as good

d Lorries climb hills more slowly

Question 18

Mark two answers

As a driver, why should you be more careful where trams operate?

a Because they do not have a horn

b Because they do not stop for cars

c Because they are silent

d Because they cannot steer to avoid you

e Because they do not have lights

Question 19

Mark one answer

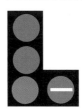

At a junction you see this signal. It means

a cars must stop

b trams must stop

c both trams and cars must stop

d both trams and cars can continue

Question 20

Mark two answers

You are travelling behind a bus that pulls up at a bus stop. What should you do?

a Accelerate past the bus sounding your horn

b Watch carefully for pedestrians

c Be ready to give way to the bus

d Pull in closely behind the bus

Question 21

Mark two answers

Why should you be careful when riding on roads where electric trams operate?

a They cannot steer to avoid you

b They move quickly and quietly

c They are noisy and slow

d They can steer to avoid you

e They give off harmful exhaust fumes

Question 22

Mark two answers

You are driving in town. Ahead of you a bus is at a bus stop. Which TWO of the following should you do?

a Be prepared to give way if the bus suddenly moves off

b Continue at the same speed but sound your horn as a warning

c Watch carefully for the sudden appearance of pedestrians

d Pass the bus as quickly as you possibly can

Question 23

Mark one answer

When you approach a bus signalling to move off from a bus stop you should

a get past before it moves

b allow it to pull away, if it is safe to do so

c flash your headlights as you approach

d signal left and wave the bus on

Question 24

Mark one answer

Which of these vehicles is LEAST likely to be affected by crosswinds?

a Cyclists

b Motorcyclists

c High-sided vehicles

d Cars

Question 25

Mark one answer

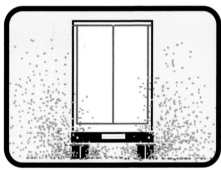

You are following a large lorry on a wet road. Spray makes it difficult to see. You should

a drop back until you can see better

b put your headlights on full beam

c keep close to the lorry, away from the spray

d speed up and overtake quickly

Question 26

Mark two answers

You are driving in heavy traffic on a wet road. Spray makes it difficult to be seen. You should use your

a full beam headlights

b rear fog lights if visibility is less than 100 metres (328 feet)

c rear fog lights if visibility is more than 100 metres (328 feet)

d dipped headlights

e side lights only

Question 27

Mark one answer

Some two-way roads are divided into three lanes. Why are these particularly dangerous?

a Traffic in both directions can use the middle lane to overtake

b Traffic can travel faster in poor weather conditions

c Traffic can overtake on the left

d Traffic uses the middle lane for emergencies only

Question 28

Mark one answer

You are driving along this road. What should you be prepared to do?

a Sound your horn and continue

b Slow down and give way

c Report the driver to the police

d Squeeze through the gap

Question 29

Mark one answer

What should you do as you approach this lorry?

a Slow down and be prepared to wait

b Make the lorry wait for you

c Flash your lights at the lorry

d Move to the right-hand side of the road

Answers and explanations

Q001 c The large articulated vehicle may need to position to the right in order to turn left into the narrow road.

Q002 b

Q003 b

Q004 b Water on metal is a dangerous combination, especially for a two-wheeled vehicle.

Q005 b Let the motorcyclist complete the overtake before even thinking about following.

Q006 b Motorcycles may have problems with strong crosswinds.

Q007 a The motorcyclist may wobble as you pass by in a windy situation.

Q008 c

Q009 a

Q010 b

Q011 b Long vehicles require more space to turn and often need to position for this.

Q012 d

Q013 b

Q014 b

Q015 d

Q016 b

Q017 a Overtaking takes time, so the longer the vehicle you overtake the greater the danger, as you will take longer to pass it.

Q018 c, d

Q019 b

Q020 b, c

Q021 a, b

Q022 a, c

Q023 b This helps traffic flow without giving confusing signals.

Q024 d Of the four mentioned, cars are by far the most stable and least affected by crosswinds.

Q025 a

Q026 b, d

Q027 a

Q028 b

Q029 a

Theory Test Questions

2001/2002

Vehicle Handling

BSM
We won't fail you

Question 1

Mark one answer

You are driving down a long, steep hill. You suddenly notice your brakes are not working as well as normal. What is the usual cause of this?

a The brakes overheating
b Air in the brake fluid
c Oil on the brakes
d Badly adjusted brakes

Question 2

Mark one answer

Riding with the side stand down could cause an accident. This is most likely to happen when

a going uphill
b accelerating
c braking
d cornering

Question 3

Mark one answer

Pressing the clutch pedal down or rolling in neutral for too long while driving will

a use more fuel
b cause the engine to overheat
c reduce your control
d improve tyre wear

Question 4

Mark one answer

You leave the choke on for too long. This could make the engine run faster than normal. This will make your motorcycle

a handle much better
b corner much safer
c stop much more quickly
d more difficult to control

Question 5

Mark one answer

How can you use the engine of your vehicle to control your speed?

a By changing to a lower gear
b By selecting reverse gear
c By changing to a higher gear
d By selecting neutral

Question 6

Mark one answer

You leave the choke on for too long. This causes the engine to run too fast. When is this likely to make your motorcycle most difficult to control?

a Accelerating

b Going uphill

c Slowing down

d On motorways

Question 7

Mark one answer

You are driving down a steep hill. Why could keeping the clutch down or selecting neutral for too long be dangerous?

a Fuel consumption will be higher

b Your vehicle will pick up speed

c It will damage the engine

d It will wear tyres out more quickly

Question 8

Mark one answer

You should NOT look down at the front wheel when riding because it can

a make your steering lighter

b improve your balance

c use less fuel

d upset your balance

Question 9

Mark one answer

Why could keeping the clutch down or selecting neutral for long periods of time be dangerous?

a Fuel spillage will occur

b Engine damage may be caused

c You will have less steering and braking control

d It will wear tyres out more quiokly

Question 10

Mark one answer

You are entering a bend. Your side stand is not fully raised. This could

a cause an accident

b improve your balance

c alter the motorcycle's centre of gravity

d make the motorcycle more stable

Question 11

Mark one answer

Why should you always reduce your speed when travelling in fog?

a Because the brakes do not work as well

b Because you could be dazzled by other people's fog lights

c Because the engine is colder

d Because it is more difficult to see events ahead

Question 12

Mark one answer

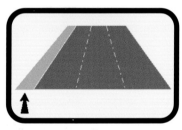

You are on a motorway in fog. The left-hand edge of the motorway can be identified by reflective studs.
What colour are they?

a Green

b Amber

c Red

d White

Question 13

Mark one answer

You are on a motorway at night.
You MUST have your headlights switched on unless

a there are vehicles close in front of you

b you are travelling below 50 mph

c the motorway is lit

d your vehicle is broken down on the hard shoulder

Question 14

Mark two answers

A rumble device is designed to

a give directions

b prevent cattle escaping

c alert you to low tyre pressure

d alert you to a hazard

e encourage you to reduce speed

Question 15

Mark one answer

You are driving on an icy road.
What distance should you drive from the car in front?

a four times the normal distance

b six times the normal distance

c eight times the normal distance

d ten times the normal distance

Question 16

Mark one answer

Why should you test your brakes after this hazard?

a Because you will be on a slippery road

b Because your brakes will be soaking wet

c Because you will have gone down a long hill

d Because you will have just crossed a long bridge

Question 17

Mark one answer

You have to make a journey in foggy conditions. You should

a follow other vehicles' tail lights closely

b avoid using dipped headlights

c leave plenty of time for your journey

d keep two seconds behind other vehicles

Question 18

Mark one answer

You are on a well-lit motorway at night. You must

a use only your sidelights

b always use your headlights

c always use rear fog lights

d use headlights only in bad weather

Question 19

Mark one answer

You are on a motorway at night with other vehicles just ahead of you. Which lights should you have on?

a Front fog lights

b Main beam headlights

c Sidelights only

d Dipped headlights

Question 20

Mark three answers

Which THREE of the following will affect your stopping distance?

a How fast you are going

b The tyres on your vehicle/motorcycle

c The time of day

d The weather

e The street lighting

Question 21

Mark one answer

You are overtaking a car at night. You must be sure that

a you flash your headlights before overtaking

b you select a higher gear

c you have switched your lights to full beam before overtaking

d you do not dazzle other road users

Question 22

Mark one answer

You are on a motorway at night. You MUST have your headlights switched on unless

a there are vehicles close in front of you

b you are travelling below 50 mph

c the motorway is lit

d your motorcycle is broken down on the hard shoulder

Question 23

Mark one answer

You see a vehicle coming towards you on a single-track road. You should

a go back to the main road

b do an emergency stop

c stop at a passing place

d put on your hazard warning lights

Question 24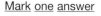

Mark one answer

You are on a narrow road at night. A slower-moving vehicle ahead has been signalling right for some time. What should you do?

a Overtake on the left

b Flash your headlights before overtaking

c Signal right and sound your horn

d Wait for the signal to be cancelled before overtaking

Question 25

Mark one answer

You have to park on the road in fog. You should

a leave parking lights on

b leave no lights on

c leave dipped headlights on

d leave main beam headlights on

Question 26

Mark one answer

You are following other vehicles in fog with your lights on. How else can you reduce the chances of being involved in an accident?

a Keep close to the vehicle in front

b Use your main beam instead of dipped headlights

c Keep together with the faster vehicles

d Reduce your speed and increase the gap

Question 27

Mark one answer

To gain basic skills in how to ride a motorcycle you should

a practise off-road with an approved training body

b ride on the road on the first dry day

c practise off-road in a public park or in a quiet cul-de-sac

d ride on the road as soon as possible

Question 28

Mark two answers

What are TWO main reasons why coasting downhill is wrong?

a Fuel consumption will be higher

b The vehicle will pick up speed

c It puts more wear and tear on the tyres

d You have less braking and steering control

e It damages the engine

Question 29

Mark one answer

When you are seated on a stationary motorcycle, your position should allow you to

a just touch the ground with your toes

b place both feet on the ground

c operate the centre stand

d reach the switches by stretching

Question 30

Mark one answer

Why is coasting wrong?

a It will cause the car to skid

b It will make the engine stall

c The engine will run faster

d There is no engine braking

Question 31

Mark two answers

As a safety measure before starting your engine, you should

a push the motorcycle forward to check the rear wheel turns freely

b engage first gear and apply the rear brake

c engage first gear and apply the front brake

d glance at the neutral light on your instrument panel

Question 32

Mark two answers

Hills can affect the performance of your vehicle. Which TWO apply when driving up steep hills?

a Higher gears will pull better

b You will slow down sooner

c Overtaking will be easier

d The engine will work harder

e The steering will feel heavier

Question 33

Mark one answer

You should not ride with your clutch lever pulled in for longer than necessary because it

a increases wear on the gearbox

b increases petrol consumption

c reduces your control of the motorcycle

d reduces the grip of the tyres

Question 34

Mark <u>one</u> answer

You are following a vehicle at a safe distance on a wet road. Another driver overtakes you and pulls into the gap you have left. What should you do?

a Flash your headlights as a warning

b Try to overtake safely as soon as you can

c Drop back to regain a safe distance

d Stay close to the other vehicle until it moves on

Question 35

Mark <u>one</u> answer

In normal riding conditions you should brake

a by using the rear brake first and then the front

b when the motorcycle is being turned or ridden through a bend

c by pulling in the clutch before using the front brake

d when the motorcycle is upright and moving in a straight line

Question 36

Mark <u>three</u> answers

In which THREE of these situations may you overtake another vehicle on the left?

a When you are in a one-way street

b When approaching a motorway slip road where you will be turning off

c When the vehicle in front is signalling to turn right

d When a slower vehicle is travelling in the right-hand lane of a dual carriageway

e In slow-moving traffic queues when traffic in the right-hand lane is moving more slowly

Question 37

Mark <u>one</u> answer

You are driving on the motorway in windy conditions. When passing high-sided vehicles you should

a increase your speed

b be wary of a sudden gust

c drive alongside very closely

d expect normal conditions

Question 38

Mark <u>one</u> answer

When coming to a normal stop on a motorcycle, you should

a only apply the front brake

b rely just on the rear brake

c apply both brakes smoothly

d apply either of the brakes gently

Question 39

Mark one answer

You are travelling in very heavy rain. Your overall stopping distance is likely to be

a doubled

b halved

c up to ten times greater

d no different

Question 40

Mark one answer

To correct a rear-wheel skid you should

a not steer at all

b steer away from it

c steer into it

d apply your handbrake

Question 41

Mark two answers

You are approaching this junction. As the motorcyclist you should

a prepare to slow down

b sound your horn

c keep near the left kerb

d speed up to clear the junction

e stop, as the car has right of way

Question 42

Mark one answer

When snow is falling heavily you should

a drive provided you use your headlights

b not drive unless you have a mobile phone

c drive only when your journey is short

d not drive unless it is essential

Question 43

Mark one answer

What can you do to improve your safety on the road as a motorcyclist?

a Anticipate the actions of others

b Stay just above the speed limits

c Keep positioned close to the kerbs

d Remain well below speed limits

Question 44

Mark one answer

You are driving in very wet weather. Your vehicle begins to slide. This effect is called

a hosing

b weaving

c aquaplaning

d fading

Question 45

Mark <u>four</u> answers

Which FOUR types of road surface increase the risk of skidding for motorcyclists?

a White lines

b Dry tarmac

c Tar banding

d Yellow grid lines

e Loose chippings

Question 46

Mark <u>two</u> answers

You have to make a journey in fog. What are the TWO most important things you should do before you set out?

a Top up the radiator with antifreeze

b Make sure that you have a warning triangle in the vehicle

c Check that your lights are working

d Check the battery

e Make sure that the windows are clean

Question 47

Mark <u>one</u> answer

Front fog lights may be used ONLY if

a visibility is seriously reduced

b they are fitted above the bumper

c they are not as bright as the headlights

d an audible warning device is used

Question 48

Mark <u>one</u> answer

Front fog lights may be used ONLY if

a your headlights are not working

b they are operated with rear fog lights

c they were fitted by the vehicle manufacturer

d visibility is seriously reduced

Question 49

Mark <u>one</u> answer

You may drive with front fog lights switched on

a when visibility is less than 100 metres (328 feet)

b at any time to be noticed

c instead of headlights on high speed roads

d when dazzled by the lights of oncoming vehicles

Question 50

Mark <u>one</u> <u>answer</u>

Front fog lights should be used ONLY when

<u>a</u> travelling in very light rain

<u>b</u> visibility is seriously reduced

<u>c</u> daylight is fading

<u>d</u> driving after midnight

Question 51

Mark <u>one</u> <u>answer</u>

Front fog lights should be used

<u>a</u> when visibility is reduced to 100 metres (328 feet)

<u>b</u> as a warning to oncoming traffic

<u>c</u> when driving during the hours of darkness

<u>d</u> in any conditions and at any time

Question 52

Mark <u>two</u> <u>answers</u>

You have to make a journey in fog. What are the TWO most important things you should do before you set out?

<u>a</u> Fill up with fuel

<u>b</u> Make sure that you have a warm drink with you

<u>c</u> Check that your lights are working

<u>d</u> Check the battery

<u>e</u> Make sure that your visor is clean

Question 53

Mark <u>one</u> <u>answer</u>

Using front fog lights in clear daylight will

<u>a</u> flatten the battery

<u>b</u> dazzle other drivers

<u>c</u> improve your visibility

<u>d</u> increase your awareness

Question 54

Mark <u>one</u> <u>answer</u>

You may use front fog lights with headlights ONLY when visibility is reduced to less than

<u>a</u> 100 metres (328 feet)

<u>b</u> 200 metres (656 feet)

<u>c</u> 300 metres (984 feet)

<u>d</u> 400 metres (1312 feet)

Question 55

Mark <u>one</u> <u>answer</u>

You are driving in fog. Why should you keep well back from the vehicle in front?

<u>a</u> In case it changes direction suddenly

<u>b</u> In case its fog lights dazzle you

<u>c</u> In case it stops suddenly

<u>d</u> In case its brake lights dazzle you

Question 56

Mark one answer

You should switch your rear fog lights on when visibility drops below

a your overall stopping distance
b ten car lengths
c 200 metres (656 feet)
d 100 metres (328 feet)

Question 57

Mark one answer

Using rear fog lights in clear daylight will

a be useful when towing a trailer
b give extra protection
c dazzle other drivers
d make following drivers keep back

Question 58

Mark two answers

You are driving on a clear dry night with your rear fog lights switched on. This may

a reduce glare from the road surface
b make other drivers think you are braking
c give a better view of the road ahead
d dazzle following drivers
e help your indicators to be seen more clearly

Question 59

Mark two answers

Why is it dangerous to leave rear fog lights on when they are not needed?

a Brake lights are less clear
b Following drivers can be dazzled
c Electrical systems could be overloaded
d Direction indicators may not work properly
e The battery could fail

Question 60

Mark one answer

While driving, the fog clears and you can see more clearly. You must remember to

a switch off the fog lights
b reduce your speed
c switch off the demister
d close any open windows

Question 61

Mark one answer

You have just driven out of fog. Visibility is now good. You MUST

a switch off all your fog lights
b keep your rear fog lights on
c keep your front fog lights on
d leave fog lights on in case fog returns

Question 62

Mark three answers

You forget to switch off your rear fog lights when the fog has cleared. This may

a dazzle other road users

b reduce battery life

c cause brake lights to be less clear

d be breaking the law

e seriously affect engine power

Question 63

Mark one answer

You have been driving in thick fog which has now cleared. You must switch OFF your rear fog lights because

a they use a lot of power from the battery

b they make your brake lights less clear

c they will cause dazzle in your rear-view mirrors

d they may not be properly adjusted

Question 64

Mark one answer

You are driving with your front fog lights switched on. Earlier fog has now cleared. What should you do?

a Leave them on if other drivers have their lights on

b Switch them off as long as visibility remains good

c Flash them to warn oncoming traffic that it is foggy

d Drive with them on instead of your headlights

Question 65

Mark one answer

While you are driving in fog, it becomes necessary to use front fog lights. You should

a only turn them on in heavy traffic conditions

b remember not to use them on motorways

c only use them with dipped headlights

d remember to switch them off as visibility improves

Question 66

Mark one answer

You have to park on the road in fog. You should

a leave sidelights on

b leave dipped headlights and fog lights on

c leave dipped headlights on

d leave main beam headlights on

Question 67

Mark one answer

On a foggy day you unavoidably have to park your car on the road. You should

a leave your headlights on

b leave your fog lights on

c leave your sidelights on

d leave your hazard lights on

Question 68

Mark one answer

You have to brake sharply and your motorcycle starts to skid. You should

a continue braking and select a low gear

b apply the brakes harder for better grip

c select neutral and use the front brake only

d release the brakes and re-apply

Question 69

Mark three answers

Which THREE of these can cause skidding?

a Braking too gently

b Leaning too far over when cornering

c Staying upright when cornering

d Braking too hard

e Changing direction suddenly

Question 70

Mark two answers

It is very cold and the road looks wet. You cannot hear any road noise. You should

a continue riding at the same speed

b ride slower in as high a gear as possible

c ride in as low a gear as possible

d keep revving your engine

e slow down as there may be black ice

Question 71

Mark one answer

You are approaching a road with a surface of loose chippings. What should you do?

a Ride normally

b Speed up

c Slow down

d Stop suddenly

Question 72

Mark one answer

When riding a motorcycle you should wear full protective clothing

a at all times

b only on faster, open roads

c just on long journeys

d only during bad weather

Question 73

Mark one answer

The best place to park your motorcycle is

a on soft tarmac

b on bumpy ground

c on grass

d on firm, level ground

Question 74

Mark one answer

When riding in windy conditions, you should

a stay close to large vehicles

b keep your speed up

c keep your speed down

d stay close to the gutter

Question 75

Mark one answer

In normal riding, your position on the road should be

a about a foot from the kerb

b about central in your lane

c on the right of your lane

d near the centre of the road

Question 76

Mark one answer

Your motorcycle is parked on a two-way road. You should get on from the

a right and apply the rear brake

b left and leave the brakes alone

c left and apply the front brake

d right and leave the brakes alone

Question 77

Mark two answers

Why should motorcyclists ride carefully where trams operate?

a They do not give way to other traffic

b They do not have mirrors and will not see you

c They do not have lights and might be difficult to see

d The rails could affect your steering and braking

Question 78

Mark <u>one</u> <u>answer</u>

It rains after a long, dry, hot spell.
This may cause the road surface to

a be unusually slippery

b give better grip

c become covered in grit

d melt and break up

Question 79

Mark <u>three</u> <u>answers</u>

The main causes of a motorcycle
skidding are

a heavy and sharp braking

b excessive acceleration

c leaning too far when cornering

d riding in wet weather

e riding in the winter

Question 80

Mark <u>one</u> <u>answer</u>

To stop your motorcycle quickly in an
emergency you should apply

a the rear brake only

b the front brake only

c the front brake just before the rear

d the rear brake just before the front

Question 81

Mark <u>two</u> <u>answers</u>

Which TWO of the following are correct?
When overtaking at night you should

a wait until a bend so that you can see
the oncoming headlights

b sound your horn twice before moving
out

c be careful because you can see less

d beware of bends in the road ahead

e put headlights on full beam

Question 82

Mark <u>one</u> <u>answer</u>

You are travelling at night. You are
dazzled by headlights coming towards
you. You should

a pull down your sun visor

b slow down or stop

c switch on your main beam headlights

d put your hand over your eyes

Question 83

Mark <u>one</u> <u>answer</u>

You are parking on a two-way road at
night. The speed limit is 40 mph. You
should park on the

a left with sidelights on

b left with no lights on

c right with sidelights on

d right with dipped headlights on

Question 84

Mark one answer

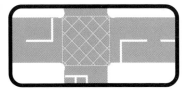

When may you wait in a box junction?

a When you are stationary in a queue of traffic
b When approaching a pelican crossing
c When approaching a zebra crossing
d When oncoming traffic prevents you turning right

Question 85

Mark four answers

Which of the following may apply when dealing with this hazard?

a It could be more difficult in winter
b Use a low gear and drive slowly
c Use a high gear to prevent wheelspin
d Test your brakes afterwards
e Always switch on fog lamps
f There may be a depth gauge

Question 86

Mark one answer

Which of these plates normally appear with this road sign?

a Humps for ½ mile
b Hump Bridge
c Low Bridge
d Soft Verge

Question 87

Mark one answer

You are on a road which has speed humps. A driver in front is travelling slower than you. You should

a sound your horn
b overtake as soon as you can
c flash your headlights
d slow down and stay behind

Question 88

Mark three answers

Areas reserved for trams may have

a metal studs around them

b white line markings

c zig zag markings

d a different coloured surface

e yellow hatch markings

f a different surface texture

Question 89

Mark one answer

Chains can be fitted to your wheels to help prevent

a damage to the road surface

b wear to the tyres

c skidding in deep snow

d the brakes locking

Question 90

Mark one answer

Traffic calming measures are used to

a stop road rage

b help overtaking

c slow traffic down

d help parking

Answers and explanations

Q001 a Selecting a lower gear before descending a long steep hill, allows the engine to control the speed of the car and helps prevent the brakes overheating. With a lower gear selected the footbrake can be used when necessary, rather than the whole time.

Q002 d

Q003 c

Q004 d

Q005 a On a long downhill slope changing to a lower gear before the descent means that you will not need to use the footbrake the whole time and will not risk the brakes overheating.

Q006 c

Q007 b

Q008 d

Q009 c

Q010 a

Q011 d Everybody knows this but an alarming number of people don't put the knowledge into practice. Accidents happen as a result.

Answers and explanations

Q012 c Red reflective studs separate the left-hand lane and the hard shoulder.

Q013 d You must use your headlights on motorways at nights even if the motorway is lit.

Q014 d, e A rumble device is normally raised strips or markings on the surface of the road.

Q015 d Stopping distances can be up to ten times longer in snow and ice. Give yourself plenty of time to stop.

Q016 b After driving through water your brakes will be wet, and wet brakes are inefficient.

Q017 c *The Highway Code* advises you to allow more time for your journey in foggy conditions. However, always ask yourself if the journey really is necessary.

Q018 b

Q019 d Full-beam headlights would dazzle the drivers in front by reflecting in their mirrors.

Q020 a, b, d

Q021 d You may need to switch to full-beam headlights as you overtake, but not before.

Q022 d

Q023 c Bear in mind that single-track roads may have passing places at long intervals. You may meet an oncoming vehicle at a point where one of you will need to reverse to the previous nearest passing point.

Q024 d

Q025 a

Q026 d

Q027 a

Q028 b, d

Q029 b

Q030 d You are coasting when you push down the clutch, disconnecting both engine and gear box.

Q031 a, d

Q032 b, d

Q033 c

Q034 c This may feel irritating, particularly if the circumstance is repeated several times. However, it is safest and, in reality, causes no delay.

Q035 d

Q036 a, c, e

Q037 b

Answers and explanations

Q038 c In good conditions you should apply greater pressure to the front brake.

Q039 a

Q040 c

Q041 a, b

Q042 d

Q043 a

Q044 c Surface water builds up a film between the road and the tyres, causing the car to drive on the film of water and not grip the road surface. The steering will feel very light if you are aquaplaning.

Q045 a, c, d, e

Q046 c, e
See and be seen are the two most crucial safety aspects of driving in fog.

Q047 a

Q048 d

Q049 a

Q050 b

Q051 a

Q052 c, e See and be seen in fog.

Q053 b

Q054 a

Q055 c If the car in front stops suddenly you may run into it if you have been driving too close.

Q056 d Remember to switch them off when visibility improves.

Q057 c Always remember to switch off your fog lights as soon as visibility improves.

Q058 b, d

Q059 a, b

Q060 a Fog lights should only be used where visibility is down to about 100 metres. Otherwise you risk dazzling other drivers.

Q061 a

Q062 a, c, d

Q063 b

Q064 b

Q065 d

Q066 a

Q067 c

Q068 d Your braking is causing the skid, so you must remove the cause by releasing the brakes and then reapplying them.

Q069 b, d, e

Q070 b, e

Q071 c

Answers and explanations

Q072 a
Q073 d
Q074 c
Q075 b Your exact position will
         depend on the width of the
         road, the road surface, your
         view ahead and any
         obstructions.
Q076 c Always mount on the side
         away from the traffic and
         apply the front brake to stop
         the motorcycle moving.
Q077 a, d
Q078 a
Q079 a, b, c
         The most common cause of
         skidding is the actions of the
         rider.

Q080 c
Q081 c, d
Q082 b
Q083 a
Q084 d You may wait in a box
         junction if your exit is clear
         but oncoming traffic prevents
         you from turning right.
Q085 a, b, d, f
Q086 a
Q087 d
Q088 b, d, f
Q089 c
Q090 c

Theory Test Questions

2001/2002

Motorway Rules

BSM
We won't fail you

Question 1

Mark one answer

You are approaching road works on a motorway. You should

a speed up to clear the works quickly

b always use the hard shoulder

c obey all speed limits

d stay very close to the vehicle in front

Question 2

Mark one answer

You are on a motorway. There is a contra flow system ahead. What would you expect to find?

a Temporary traffic lights

b Lower speed limits

c Wider lanes than normal

d Speed humps

Question 3

Mark one answer

You are joining a motorway. Why is it important to make full use of the slip road?

a Because there is space available to turn round if you need to

b To allow you direct access to the overtaking lanes

c To build up a speed similar to traffic on the motorway

d Because you can continue on the hard shoulder

Question 4

Mark one answer

You are driving on a motorway. The car ahead shows its hazard lights for a short time. This tells you that

a the driver wants you to overtake

b the other car is going to change lanes

c traffic ahead is slowing or stopping suddenly

d there is a police speed check ahead

Question 5

Mark one answer

How should you use the emergency telephone on a motorway?

a Stay close to the carriageway

b Face the oncoming traffic

c Keep your back to the traffic

d Stand on the hard shoulder

Question 6

Mark one answer

You are on a motorway. What colour are the reflective studs on the left of the carriageway?

a Green

b Red

c White

d Amber

Question 7

Mark one answer

On a three-lane motorway which lane should you normally use?

a Left

b Right

c Centre

d Either the right or centre

Question 8

Mark one answer

A basic rule when on motorways is

a use the lane that has least traffic

b keep to the left lane unless overtaking

c overtake on the side that is clearest

d try to keep above 50 mph to prevent congestion

Question 9

Mark one answer

You are driving at 70 mph on a three-lane motorway. There is no traffic ahead. Which lane should you use?

a Any lane

b Middle lane

c Right lane

d Left lane

Question 10

Mark one answer

Your vehicle has broken down on a motorway. You are not able to stop on the hard shoulder. What should you do?

a Switch on your hazard warning lights

b Stop following traffic and ask for help

c Attempt to repair your vehicle quickly

d Stand behind your vehicle to warn others

Question 11

Mark one answer

You are riding at 70 mph on a three-lane motorway. There is no traffic ahead. Which lane should you use?

a Any lane

b Middle lane

c Right lane

d Left lane

Question 12

Mark three answers

When may you stop on a motorway?

a If you have to read a map

b When you are tired and need a rest

c If red lights show above every lane

d When told to by the police

e If your mobile phone rings

f In an emergency or a breakdown

Question 13

Mark one answer

When going through a contraflow system on a motorway you should

a ensure that you do not exceed 30 mph

b keep a good distance from the vehicle ahead

c switch lanes to keep the traffic flowing

d stay close to the vehicle ahead to reduce queues

Question 14

Mark one answer

Why is it particularly important to carry out a check on your motorcycle before making a long motorway journey?

a You will have to do more harsh braking on motorways

b Motorway service stations do not deal with breakdowns

c The road surface will wear down the tyres faster

d Continuous high speeds may increase the risk of your motorcycle breaking down

Question 15

Mark one answer

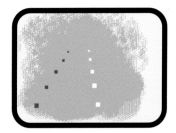

You are on a three-lane motorway. There are red reflective studs on your left and white ones to your right. Where are you?

a In the right-hand lane

b In the middle lane

c On the hard shoulder

d In the left-hand lane

Question 16

Mark one answer

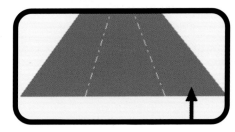

For what reason may you use the right-hand lane of a motorway?

a For keeping out of the way of lorries

b For riding at more than 70 mph

c For turning right

d For overtaking other vehicles

Question 17

Mark one answer

Why is it particularly important to carry out a check on your vehicle before making a long motorway journey?

a You will have to do more harsh braking on motorways

b Motorway service stations do not deal with breakdowns

c The road surface will wear down the tyres faster

d Continuous high speeds may increase the risk of your vehicle breaking down

Question 18

Mark one answer

The emergency telephones on a motorway are connected to the

a ambulance service

b police control

c fire brigade

d breakdown service

Question 19

Mark one answer

You are intending to leave the motorway at the next exit. Before you reach the exit you should normally position your motorcycle

a in the middle lane

b in the left-hand lane

c on the hard shoulder

d in any lane

Question 20

Mark one answer

On a motorway you may ONLY stop on the hard shoulder

a in an emergency

b if you feel tired and need to rest

c if you accidentally go past the exit that you wanted to take

d to pick up a hitchhiker

Question 21

Mark one answer

You are intending to leave the motorway at the next exit. Before you reach the exit you should normally position your vehicle

a in the middle lane

b in the left-hand lane

c on the hard shoulder

d in any lane

Question 22

Mark one answer

As a provisional licence-holder you should not drive a car

a over 50 mph

b at night

c on the motorway

d with passengers in rear seats

Question 23

Mark one answer

A motorcycle is not allowed on a motorway if it has an engine size smaller than

a 50cc

b 125cc

c 150cc

d 250cc

Question 24

Mark four answers

Which FOUR of these must NOT use motorways?

a Learner car drivers

b Motorcycles over 50cc

c Double-decker buses

d Farm tractors

e Horse riders

f Cyclists

Question 25

Mark one answer

To ride on a motorway your motorcycle must be

a 50cc or more

b 100cc or more

c 125cc or more

d 250cc or more

Question 26

Mark four answers

Which FOUR of these must NOT use motorways?

a Learner car drivers

b Motorcycles over 50cc

c Double-decker buses

d Farm tractors

e Learner motorcyclists

f Cyclists

Question 27

Mark one answer

Immediately after joining a motorway you should normally

a try to overtake

b readjust your mirrors

c position your vehicle in the centre lane

d keep in the left lane

Question 28

Mark one answer

You are joining a motorway from a slip road on the left. You should

a adjust your speed to the speed of the traffic on the motorway

b accelerate as quickly as you can and ride straight out

c ride onto the hard shoulder until a gap appears

d expect drivers on the motorway to give way to you

Question 29

Mark one answer

When joining a motorway you must always

a use the hard shoulder

b stop at the end of the acceleration lane

c come to a stop before joining the motorway

d give way to traffic already on the motorway

Question 30

Mark one answer

What is the national speed limit for cars and motorcycles in the centre lane of a three-lane motorway?

a 40 mph

b 50 mph

c 60 mph

d 70 mph

Question 31

Mark one answer

You are riding on a motorway. Unless signs show otherwise you must NOT exceed

a 50 mph

b 60 mph

c 70 mph

d 80 mph

Question 32

Mark one answer

What is the national speed limit on motorways for cars and motorcycles?

a 30 mph

b 50 mph

c 60 mph

d 70 mph

Question 33

Mark one answer

You are towing a trailer on a motorway. What is your maximum speed limit?

a 40 mph

b 50 mph

c 60 mph

d 70 mph

Question 34

Mark one answer

You are driving a car on a motorway.
Unless signs show otherwise you must
NOT exceed

a 50 mph

b 60 mph

c 70 mph

d 80 mph

Question 35

Mark one answer

On a three-lane motorway why should
you normally ride in the left lane?

a The left lane is only for lorries and
motorcycles

b The left lane should only be used by
smaller vehicles

c The lanes on the right are for
overtaking

d Motorcycles are not allowed in the far
right lane

Question 36

Mark one answer

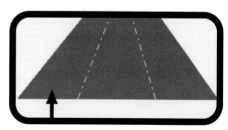

The left-hand lane on a three-lane
motorway is for use by

a any vehicle

b large vehicles only

c emergency vehicles only

d slow vehicles only

Question 37

Mark one answer

The left-hand lane of a motorway should
be used for

a breakdowns and emergencies only

b overtaking slower traffic in the other
lanes

c slow vehicles only

d normal driving

Question 38

Mark one answer

What is the right-hand lane used for on a three-lane motorway?

a Emergency vehicles only

b Overtaking

c Vehicles towing trailers

d Coaches only

Question 39

Mark one answer

Which of these is NOT allowed to travel in the right-hand lane of a three-lane motorway?

a A small delivery van

b A motorcycle

c A vehicle towing a trailer

d A motorcycle and side-car

Question 40

Mark one answer

On motorways you should never overtake on the left UNLESS

a you can see well ahead that the hard shoulder is clear

b the traffic in the right-hand lane is signalling right

c you warn drivers behind by signalling left

d there is a queue of traffic to your right that is moving more slowly

Question 41

Mark two answers

You are travelling on a motorway. You decide you need a rest. You should

a stop on the hard shoulder

b go to a service area

c park on the slip road

d park on the central reservation

e leave at the next exit

Question 42

Mark one answer

You are driving on a motorway. You have to slow down quickly due to a hazard. You should

a switch on your hazard lights

b switch on your headlights

c sound your horn

d flash your headlights

Question 43

Mark one answer

You break down on a motorway. You need to call for help. Why may it be better to use an emergency roadside telephone rather than a mobile phone?

a It connects you to a local garage

b Using a mobile phone will distract other drivers

c It allows easy location by the emergency services

d Mobile phones do not work on motorways

Question 44

Mark one answer

Your vehicle breaks down on the hard shoulder of a motorway. You decide to use your mobile phone to call for help. You should

a stand at the rear of the vehicle while making the call

b try to repair the vehicle yourself

c get out of the vehicle by the right-hand door

d check your location from the marker posts on the left

Question 45

Mark one answer

You get a puncture on the motorway. You manage to get your vehicle onto the hard shoulder. You should

a change the wheel yourself immediately

b use the emergency telephone and call for assistance

c try to wave down another vehicle for help

d only change the wheel if you have a passenger to help you

Question 46

Mark one answer

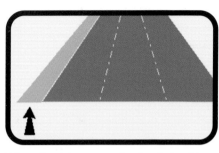

What should you use the hard shoulder of a motorway for?

a Stopping in an emergency

b Leaving the motorway

c Stopping when you are tired

d Joining the motorway

Question 47

Mark one answer

After a breakdown you need to rejoin the main carriageway of a motorway from the hard shoulder. You should

a move out onto the carriageway then build up your speed

b move out onto the carriageway using your hazard lights

c gain speed on the hard shoulder before moving out onto the carriageway

d wait on the hard shoulder until someone flashes their headlights at you

Question 48

Mark one answer

A crawler lane on a motorway is found

a on a steep gradient

b before a service area

c before a junction

d along the hard shoulder

Question 49

Mark one answer

You are allowed to stop on a motorway when you

a need to walk and get fresh air

b wish to pick up hitch hikers

c are told to do so by flashing red lights

d need to use a mobile telephone

Question 50

Mark one answer

You are on a motorway. There are red flashing lights above every lane. You must

a pull onto the hard shoulder

b slow down and watch for further signals

c leave at the next exit

d stop and wait

Question 51

Mark one answer

You are driving on a motorway. By mistake, you go past the exit that you wanted to take. You should

a carefully reverse on the hard shoulder

b carry on to the next exit

c carefully reverse in the left-hand lane

d make a U-turn at the next gap in the central reservation

Question 52

Mark one answer

You are in the right-hand lane on a motorway. You see these overhead signs. This means

a move to the left and reduce your speed to 50 mph

b there are roadworks 50 metres (55 yards) ahead

c use the hard shoulder until you have passed the hazard

d leave the motorway at the next exit

Question 53

Mark one answer

What do these motorway signs show?

a They are countdown markers to a bridge

b They are distance markers to the next telephone

c They are countdown markers to the next exit

d They warn of a police control ahead

Question 54

Mark one answer

On a motorway the amber reflective studs can be found between

a the hard shoulder and the carriageway

b the acceleration lane and the carriageway

c the central reservation and the carriageway

d each pair of the lanes

Question 55

Mark one answer

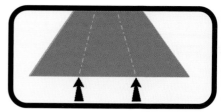

What colour are the reflective studs between the lanes on a motorway?

a Green

b Amber

c White

d Red

Question 56

Mark one answer

What colour are the reflective studs between a motorway and its slip road?

a Amber

b White

c Green

d Red

Question 57

Mark one answer

You have broken down on a motorway. To find the nearest emergency telephone you should always walk

a with the traffic flow

b facing oncoming traffic

c in the direction shown on the marker posts

d in the direction of the nearest exit

Question 58

Mark <u>one</u> <u>answer</u>

You are travelling along the left lane of a three-lane motorway. Traffic is joining from a slip road. You should

a race the other vehicles

b move to another lane

c maintain a steady speed

d switch on your hazard flashers

Question 59

Mark <u>one</u> <u>answer</u>

You are on a three-lane motorway towing a trailer. You may use the right-hand lane when

a there are lane closures

b there is slow-moving traffic

c you can maintain a high speed

d large vehicles are in the left and centre lanes

Answers and explanations

Q001   c In motorway roadworks you are sometimes, but not always, directed to use the hard shoulder, especially where the right-hand lane is closed. Therefore, 'b' is not correct. There often are lower speed limits to protect the traffic in contra flows or narrow lanes and you must obey these.

Q002   b

Q003   c You need to build up your speed to that of the traffic already on the motorway so you can ease into a gap in the flow of traffic.

Q004   c

Q005   b

Q006   b

Q007   a The other lanes should be used for overtaking.

Q008   b

Q009   d You should always use the left-hand lane for normal driving.

Q010   a

Q011   d

Q012   c, d, f
       Service areas are not officially part of the motorway.

Q013   b In these circumstances there may also be a speed limit – keep to it.

Q014   d

Q015   d

Q016   d

Q017   d Check oil and windscreen washer levels and also check the tyres. Plan your rest stops.

Q018   b

Q019   b

Q020   a

Answers and explanations

Q021	b
Q022	c
Q023	a
Q024	a, d, e, f
Q025	a
Q026	a, d, e, f
Q027	d
Q028	a The slip road gives you time and space to adjust your speed to that of the traffic on the motorway.
Q029	d
Q030	d
Q031	c
Q032	d Speed limits may be altered due to weather conditions. Look out for signs on the central reserve or above your lane.
Q033	c
Q034	c
Q035	c
Q036	a Strictly speaking, any vehicle which is allowed on a motorway.
Q037	d
Q038	b
Q039	c
Q040	d
Q041	b, e
Q042	a

Q043	c
Q044	d
Q045	b It is dangerous to attempt to change the wheel yourself. Try to keep as far from the carriageway as possible while waiting for assistance.
Q046	a You may only stop on the hard shoulder in an emergency.
Q047	c
Q048	a
Q049	c
Q050	d
Q051	b
Q052	a
Q053	c
Q054	c
Q055	c
Q056	c
Q057	c
Q058	b
Q059	a

Theory Test Questions

2001/2002

Rules of the Road

BSM

We won't fail you

Question 1

Mark one answer

When leaving your car unattended for a few minutes you should

a leave the engine running

b switch the engine off but leave the key in

c lock it and remove the key

d park near a traffic warden

Question 2

Mark one answer

When parking and leaving your car for a few minutes you should

a leave it unlocked

b lock it and remove the key

c leave the hazard warning lights on

d leave the interior light on

Question 3

Mark one answer

When leaving your car, to help keep it secure you should

a leave the hazard warning lights on

b lock it and remove the key

c park on a one-way street

d park in a residential area

Question 4

Mark one answer

When leaving your vehicle, where should you park if possible?

a Opposite a traffic island

b In a secure car park

c On a bend

d At or near a taxi rank

Question 5

Mark one answer

Where is the safest place to park your vehicle at night?

a In a garage

b On a busy road

c In a quiet car park

d Near a red route

Question 6

Mark one answer

You are away from home and have to park your vehicle overnight. Where should you leave it?

a Opposite another parked vehicle

b In a quiet road

c Opposite a traffic island

d In a secure car park

Question 7

Mark one answer

To help keep your vehicle secure at night where should you park?

a Near a police station

b In a quiet road

c On a red route

d In a well lit area

Question 8

Mark one answer

You are leaving your motorcycle parked on a road. When may you leave the engine running?

a If you will be parked for less than five minutes

b If the battery is flat

c When in a 20 mph zone

d Not on any occasion

Question 9

Mark one answer

You are intending to turn right at a crossroads. An oncoming driver is also turning right. It will normally be safer to

a keep the other vehicle to your RIGHT and turn behind it (offside to offside)

b keep the other vehicle to your LEFT and turn in front of it (nearside to nearside)

c carry on and turn at the next junction instead

d hold back and wait for the other driver to turn first

Question 10

Mark one answer

You are on a road that has no traffic signs. There are street lights. What is the speed limit?

a 20 mph

b 30 mph

c 40 mph

d 60 mph

Question 11

Mark three answers

You are going along a street with parked vehicles on the left-hand side. For which THREE reasons should you keep your speed down?

a So that oncoming traffic can see you more clearly

b You may set off car alarms

c Vehicles may be pulling out

d Drivers' doors may open

e Children may run out from between the vehicles

Question 12

Mark one answer

You are looking for somewhere to park your motorcycle. The area is full EXCEPT for spaces marked 'disabled use'. You can

a use these spaces when elsewhere is full

b park if you stay with your motorcycle

c use these spaces, disabled or not

d not park there unless permitted

Question 13

Mark <u>one</u> <u>answer</u>

You meet an obstruction on your side of the road. You should

a carry on, you have priority

b give way to oncoming traffic

c wave oncoming vehicles through

d accelerate to get past first

Question 14

Mark <u>one</u> <u>answer</u>

Your motorcycle is parked on the road at night. When must you use sidelights?

a Where there are continuous white lines in the middle of the road

b Where the speed limit exceeds 30 mph

c Where you are facing oncoming traffic

d Where you are near a bus stop

Question 15

Mark <u>two</u> <u>answers</u>

You are on a two-lane dual carriageway. For which TWO of the following would you use the right-hand lane?

a Turning right

b Normal progress

c Staying at the minimum allowed speed

d Constant high speed

e Overtaking slower traffic

f Mending punctures

Question 16

Mark <u>one</u> <u>answer</u>

Who has priority at an unmarked crossroads?

a The larger vehicle

b No one has priority

c The faster vehicle

d The smaller vehicle

Question 17

Mark <u>one</u> <u>answer</u>

You are in the right-hand lane of a dual carriageway. You see signs showing that the right lane is closed 800 yards ahead. You should

a keep in that lane until you reach the queue

b move to the left immediately

c wait and see which lane is moving faster

d move to the left in good time

Question 18

Mark one answer

You are on a road with passing places. It is only wide enough for one vehicle. There is a car coming towards you. What should you do?

a Pull into a passing place on your right

b Force the other driver to reverse

c Turn round and ride back to the main road

d Pull into a passing place on your left

Question 19

Mark one answer

You are riding slowly in a town centre. Before turning left you should glance over your left shoulder to

a check for cyclists

b help keep your balance

c look for traffic signs

d check for potholes

Question 20

Mark one answer

You are leaving your vehicle parked on a road. When may you leave the engine running?

a If you will be parked for less than five minutes

b If the battery is flat

c When in a 20 mph zone

d Not on any occasion

Question 21

Mark one answer

What is the nearest you may park to a junction?

a 10 metres (32 feet)

b 12 metres (39 feet)

c 15 metres (49 feet)

d 20 metres (66 feet)

Question 22

Mark three answers

In which THREE places must you NOT park?

a Near the brow of a hill

b At or near a bus stop

c Where there is no pavement

d Within 10 metres (32 feet) of a junction

e On a 40 mph road

Question 23

Mark one answer

You are looking for somewhere to park your vehicle. The area is full EXCEPT for spaces marked 'disabled use'. You can

a use these spaces when elsewhere is full

b park if you stay with your vehicle

c use these spaces, disabled or not

d not park there unless permitted

Question 24

Mark one answer

Your vehicle is parked on the road at night. When must you use sidelights?

a Where there are continuous white lines in the middle of the road

b Where the speed limit exceeds 30 mph

c Where you are facing oncoming traffic

d Where you are near a bus stop

Question 25

Mark one answer

You are waiting at a level crossing. A train has passed but the lights keep flashing. You must

a carry on waiting

b phone the signal operator

c edge over the stop line and look for trains

d park and investigate

Question 26

Mark one answer

DISABLED

What MUST you have to park in a disabled space?

a An orange or blue badge

b A wheelchair

c An advanced driver certificate

d A modified vehicle

Question 27

Mark one answer

You are driving at night with full beam headlights on. A vehicle is overtaking you. You should dip your lights

a some time after the vehicle has passed you

b before the vehicle starts to pass you

c only if the other driver dips their headlights

d as soon as the vehicle passes you

Question 28

Mark one answer

You may drive over a footpath

a to overtake slow-moving traffic

b when the pavement is very wide

c if no pedestrians are near

d to get into a property

Question 29

Mark one answer

What is the meaning of this sign?

a Local speed limit applies

b No waiting on the carriageway

c National speed limit applies

d No entry to vehicular traffic

Question 30

Mark one answer

What is the national speed limit on a single carriageway road for cars and motorcycles?

a 70 mph
b 60 mph
c 50 mph
d 30 mph

Question 31

Mark one answer

What is the national speed limit for cars and motorcycles on a dual carriageway?

a 30 mph
b 50 mph
c 60 mph
d 70 mph

Question 32

Mark one answer

A single carriageway road has this sign. What is the maximum permitted speed for a car towing a trailer?

a 30 mph
b 40 mph
c 50 mph
d 60 mph

Question 33

Mark one answer

There are no speed limit signs on the road. How is a 30 mph limit indicated?

a By hazard warning lines
b By street lighting
c By pedestrian islands
d By double or single yellow lines

Question 34

Mark one answer

Where you see street lights but no speed limit signs the limit is usually

a 30 mph
b 40 mph
c 50 mph
d 60 mph

Question 35

Mark one answer

You are towing a small caravan on a dual carriageway. You must not exceed

a 50 mph
b 40 mph
c 70 mph
d 60 mph

Question 36

Mark one answer

You are riding on a busy dual carriageway. When changing lanes you should

a rely totally on mirrors

b always increase your speed

c signal so others will give way

d use mirrors and shoulder checks

Question 37

Mark one answer

What does this sign mean?

a Minimum speed 30 mph

b End of maximum speed

c End of minimum speed

d Maximum speed 30 mph

Question 38

Mark one answer

There is a tractor ahead of you. You wish to overtake but you are NOT sure if it is safe to do so. You should

a follow another overtaking vehicle through

b sound your horn to the slow vehicle to pull over

c speed through but flash your lights to oncoming traffic

d not overtake if you are in doubt

Question 39

Mark two answers

As a motorcycle rider which TWO lanes must you NOT use?

a Crawler lane

b Overtaking lane

c Acceleration lane

d Cycle lane

e Tram lane

Question 40

Mark three answers

Which three of the following are most likely to take an unusual course at roundabouts?

a Horse riders

b Milk floats

c Delivery vans

d Long vehicles

e Estate cars

f Cyclists

Question 41

Mark four answers

In which FOUR places must you NOT park or wait?

a On a dual carriageway
b At a bus stop
c On the slope of a hill
d Opposite a traffic island
e In front of someone else's drive
f On the brow of a hill

Question 42

Mark one answer

You are finding it difficult to find a parking place in a busy town. You can see there is space on the zigzag lines of a zebra crossing. Can you park there?

a No, unless you stay with your car
b Yes, in order to drop off a passenger
c Yes, if you do not block people from crossing
d No, not in any circumstances

Question 43

Mark two answers

In which TWO places must you NOT park?

a Near a school entrance
b Near a police station
c In a side road
d At a bus stop
e In a one-way street

Question 44

Mark one answer

On a clearway you must not stop

a at any time
b when it is busy
c in the rush hour
d during daylight hours

Question 45

Mark one answer

You are driving on an urban clearway. You may stop only to

a set down and pick up passengers
b use a mobile telephone
c ask for directions
d load or unload goods

Question 46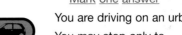

Mark one answer

Meter
ZONE

No loading

Mon - Fri
8.30 am - 6.30 pm
Saturday
8.30 am - 1.30 pm

You want to park and you see this sign. On the days and times shown you should

a park in a bay and not pay
b park on yellow lines and pay
c park on yellow lines and not pay
d park in a bay and pay

Question 47

Mark one answer

You are turning right at a large roundabout. Just before you leave the roundabout you should

a take a 'lifesaver' glance over your left shoulder

b take a 'lifesaver' glance over your right shoulder

c put on your right indicator

d cancel the left indicator

Question 48

Mark one answer

What is the meaning of this sign?

a No entry

b Waiting restrictions

c National speed limit

d School crossing patrol

Question 49

Mark one answer

You park overnight on a road with a 40 mph speed limit. You should

a park facing the traffic

b park with sidelights on

c park with dipped headlights on

d park near a street light

Question 50

Mark three answers

When filtering through slow-moving or stationary traffic you should

a watch for hidden vehicles emerging from side roads

b continually use your horn as a warning

c look for vehicles changing course suddenly

d always ride with your hazard lights on

e stand up on the footrests for a good view ahead

f look for pedestrians walking between vehicles

Question 51

Mark one answer

You can park on the right-hand side of a road at night

a in a one-way street

b with your sidelights on

c more than 10 metres (32 feet) from a junction

d under a lamp-post

Question 52

Mark one answer

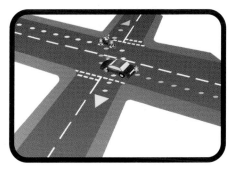

You are both turning right at these crossroads. It is safer to keep the car to your right so you can

a see approaching traffic

b keep close to the kerb

c keep clear of following traffic

d make oncoming vehicles stop

Question 53

Mark one answer

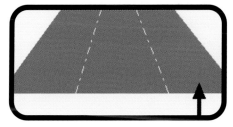

On a three-lane dual carriageway the right-hand lane can be used for

a overtaking only, never turning right

b overtaking or turning right

c fast-moving traffic only

d turning right only, never overtaking

Question 54

Mark one answer

You are entering an area of roadworks. There is a temporary speed limit displayed. You must

a not exceed the speed limit

b obey the limit only during rush hour

c accept the speed limit as advisable

d obey the limit except for overnight

Question 55

Mark one answer

You may drive a motor car in this bus lane

a outside its operation hours

b to get to the front of a traffic queue

c at no times at all

d to overtake slow-moving traffic

Question 56

Mark one answer

While driving, you approach roadworks. You see a temporary maximum speed limit sign. You must

a comply with the sign during the working day

b comply with the sign at all times

c comply with the sign when the lanes are narrow

d comply with the sign during the hours of darkness

Question 57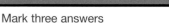

Mark three answers

On which THREE occasions MUST you stop your motorcycle?

a When involved in an accident

b At a red traffic light

c When signalled to do so by a police officer

d At a junction with double broken white lines

e At a pelican crossing when the amber light is flashing and no pedestrians are crossing

Question 58

Mark three answers

As a car driver which THREE lanes are you NOT normally allowed to use?

a Crawler lane

b Bus lane

c Overtaking lane

d Acceleration lane

e Cycle lane

f Tram lane

Question 59

Mark two answers

You are driving on a road that has a cycle lane. The lane is marked by a broken white line. This means that

a you should not drive in the lane unless it is unavoidable

b you should not park in the lane unless it is unavoidable

c you can drive in the lane at any time

d the lane must be used by motorcyclists in heavy traffic

Question 60

Mark one answer

You are driving along a road that has a cycle lane. The lane is marked by a solid white line. This means that during its period of operation

a the lane may be used for car parking

b you may drive in that lane at any time

c the lane may be used when necessary

d you must not drive in that lane

Question 61

Mark one answer

A cycle lane is marked by a solid white line. You must not drive or park in it

a at any time

b during the rush hour

c if a cyclist is using it

d during its period of operation

Question 62

Mark one answer

You are approaching a busy junction. There are several lanes with road markings. At the last moment you realise that you are in the wrong lane. You should

a continue in that lane

b force your way across

c stop until the area has cleared

d use clear arm signals to cut across

Question 63

Mark one answer

Where may you overtake on a one-way street?

a Only on the left-hand side

b Overtaking is not allowed

c Only on the right-hand side

d Either on the right or the left

Question 64

Mark one answer

You are on a road that is only wide enough for one vehicle. There is a car coming towards you. What should you do?

a Pull into a passing place on your right

b Force the other driver to reverse

c Pull into a passing place if your vehicle is wider

d Pull into a passing place on your left

Question 65

Mark one answer

Signals are normally given by direction indicators and

a brake lights

b side lights

c fog lights

d interior lights

Question 66

Mark one answer

When going straight ahead at a roundabout you should

a indicate left before leaving the roundabout

b not indicate at any time

c indicate right when approaching the roundabout

d indicate left when approaching the roundabout

Question 67

Mark <u>one</u> <u>answer</u>

You want to tow a trailer with your motorcycle. Your engine must be more than

a 50cc

b 125cc

c 525cc

d 1000cc

Question 68

Mark <u>one</u> <u>answer</u>

Which vehicle might have to use a different course to normal at roundabouts?

a Sports car

b Van

c Estate car

d Long vehicle

Question 69

Mark <u>one</u> <u>answer</u>

What is the national speed limit on a single carriageway?

a 40 mph

b 50 mph

c 60 mph

d 70 mph

Question 70

Mark <u>one</u> <u>answer</u>

You are going straight ahead at a roundabout. How should you signal?

a Signal right on the approach and then left to leave the roundabout

b Signal left as you leave the roundabout

c Signal left on the approach to the roundabout and keep the signal on until you leave

d Signal left just after you pass the exit before the one you will take

Question 71

Mark <u>one</u> <u>answer</u>

What does this sign mean?

a No parking for solo motorcycles

b Parking for solo motorcycles

c Passing place for motorcycles

d Police motorcycles only

Question 72

Mark one answer

At a crossroads there are no signs or road markings. Two vehicles approach. Which has priority?

a Neither vehicle

b The vehicle travelling the fastest

c The vehicle on the widest road

d Vehicles approaching from the right

Question 73

Mark three answers

Your motorcycle will be parked for a long time. You should

a use the centre stand if fitted

b park on a wide pavement

c lean it against a wall

d switch off the fuel tap

e park where the ground is firm and level

f park with your lights on in daytime

Question 74

Mark one answer

The dual carriageway you are turning right onto has a narrow central reserve. You should

a proceed to central reserve and wait

b wait until the road is clear in both directions

c stop in first lane so that other vehicles give way

d emerge slightly to show your intentions

Question 75

Mark one answer

You are riding towards road works. The temporary traffic lights are at red. The road ahead is clear. What should you do?

a Ride on with extreme caution

b Ride on at normal speed

c Carry on if approaching cars have stopped

d Wait for the green light

Question 76

Mark one answer

While driving, you intend to turn left into a minor road. On the approach you should

a keep just left of the middle of the road

b keep in the middle of the road

c swing out wide just before turning

d keep well to the left of the road

Question 77

Mark one answer

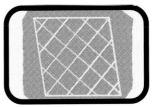

You may only enter a box junction when

a there are less than two vehicles in front of you

b the traffic lights show green

c your exit road is clear

d you need to turn left

Question 78

Mark one answer

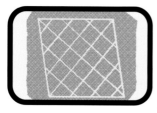

You may wait in a yellow box junction when

a oncoming traffic is preventing you from turning right

b you are in a queue of traffic turning left

c you are in a queue of traffic to go ahead

d you are on a roundabout

Question 79

Mark one answer

You want to turn right at a box junction. There is oncoming traffic. You should

a wait in the box junction if your exit is clear

b wait before the junction until it is clear of all traffic

c drive on, you cannot turn right at a box junction

d drive slowly into the box junction when signalled by oncoming traffic

Question 80

Mark three answers

On which THREE occasions MUST you stop your vehicle?

a When involved in an accident

b At a red traffic light

c When signalled to do so by a police officer

d At a junction with double broken white lines

e At a pelican crossing when the amber light is flashing and no pedestrians are crossing

Question 81

Mark three answers

You MUST stop when signalled to do so by which THREE of these?

a A police officer

b A pedestrian

c A school crossing patrol

d A bus driver

e A red traffic light

Question 82

Mark three answers

At roadworks which of the following can control traffic flow?

a A STOP–GO board

b Flashing amber lights

c A policeman

d Flashing red lights

e Temporary traffic lights

Question 83

Mark one answer

You are waiting at a level crossing. The red warning lights continue to flash after a train has passed by. What should you do?

a Get out and investigate

b Telephone the signal operator

c Continue to wait

d Drive across carefully

Question 84

Mark one answer

You are driving over a level crossing. The warning lights come on and a bell rings. What should you do?

a Get everyone out of the vehicle immediately

b Stop and reverse back to clear the crossing

c Keep going and clear the crossing

d Stop immediately and use your hazard warning lights

Question 85

Mark one answer

You will see these markers when approaching

a the end of a motorway

b a concealed level crossing

c a concealed speed limit sign

d the end of a dual carriageway

Question 86

Mark one answer

Someone is waiting to cross at a zebra crossing. They are standing on the pavement. You should normally

a go on quickly boforo thoy otop onto the crossing

b stop before you reach the zigzag lines and let them cross

c stop, let them cross, wait patiently

d ignore them as they are still on the pavement

Question 87

Mark one answer

At toucan crossings, apart from pedestrians you should be aware of

a emergency vehicles emerging

b buses pulling out

c trams crossing in front

d cyclists riding across

Question 88

Mark <u>two</u> <u>answers</u>

Who can use a toucan crossing?

a Trains

b Cyclists

c Buses

d Pedestrians

e Trams

Question 89

Mark <u>one</u> <u>answer</u>

At a pelican crossing, what does a flashing amber light mean?

<u>a</u> You must not move off until the lights stop flashing

<u>b</u> You must give way to pedestrians still on the crossing

<u>c</u> You can move off, even if pedestrians are still on the crossing

<u>d</u> You must stop because the lights are about to change to red

Question 90

Mark <u>one</u> <u>answer</u>

You are waiting at a pelican crossing. The red light changes to flashing amber. This means you must

<u>a</u> wait for pedestrians on the crossing to clear

<u>b</u> move off immediately without any hesitation

<u>c</u> wait for the green light before moving off

<u>d</u> get ready and go when the continuous amber light shows

Question 91

Mark <u>one</u> <u>answer</u>

You are on a busy main road and find that you are travelling in the wrong direction. What should you do?

<u>a</u> Turn into a side road on the right and reverse into the main road

<u>b</u> Make a U-turn in the main road

<u>c</u> Make a 'three-point' turn in the main road

<u>d</u> Turn round in a side road

Question 92

Mark <u>one</u> <u>answer</u>

You may remove your seat belt when carrying out a manoeuvre that involves

a reversing

b a hill start

c an emergency stop

d driving slowly

Question 93

Mark <u>one</u> <u>answer</u>

When can you park on the left opposite these road markings?

a If the line nearest to you is broken

b When there are no yellow lines

c To pick up or set down passengers

d During daylight hours only

Question 94

Mark one answer

You must not reverse

a for longer than necessary

b for more than a car's length

c into a side road

d in a built-up area

Question 95

Mark one answer

You are parked in a busy high street. What is the safest way to turn your vehicle around to go the opposite way?

a Find a quiet side road to turn round in

b Drive into a side road and reverse into the main road

c Get someone to stop the traffic

d Do a U-turn

Question 96

Mark one answer

When you are NOT sure that it is safe to reverse your vehicle you should

a use your horn

b rev your engine

c get out and check

d reverse slowly

Question 97

Mark one answer

When may you reverse from a side road into a main road?

a Only if both roads are clear of traffic

b Not at any time

c At any time

d Only if the main road is clear of traffic

Question 98

Mark one answer

You are reversing your vehicle into a side road. When would the greatest hazard to passing traffic occur?

a After you've completed the manoeuvre

b Just before you actually begin to manoeuvre

c After you've entered the side road

d When the front of your vehicle swings out

Question 99

Mark one answer

You are travelling on a well-lit road at night in a built-up area. By using dipped headlights you will be able to

a see further along the road

b go at a much faster speed

c switch to main beam quickly

d be easily seen by others

Answers and explanations

Q001 c Never risk leaving your car unattended with the key in. An opportunist might come along and steal it.

Q002 b

Q003 b

Q004 b

Q005 a

Q006 d In particular, you should avoid leaving your car unattended in poorly lit areas, especially if they are high risk.

Q007 d

Q008 d

Q009 a

Q010 b If there are street lights, the speed limit is 30 mph unless a road sign states otherwise.

Q011 c, d, e

Q012 d

Q013 b

Q014 b

Q015 a, e

Q016 b An unmarked crossroads has no road signs or road markings and no vehicle has priority even if one road is wider or busier than the other.

Q017 d

Q018 d

Q019 a

Q020 d

Q021 a

Q022 a, b, d

Q023 d

Q024 b

Q025 a

Q026 a Since 1 April 2000 the Orange Badge scheme has been known as the Blue Badge scheme.

Q027 d If you dip your lights too early you may reduce your vision; too late and you may dazzle the driver who has overtaken.

Q028 d

Q029 c

Q030 b

Q031 d The national speed limit is 70 mph on a motorway or dual carriageway and 60 mph on two-way roads unless traffic signs denote anything different.

Q032 c

Q033 b

Q034 a

Q035 d

Q036 d A shoulder check allows you to see a vehicle that may be in your blindspot.

Answers and explanations

Q037	c
Q038	d
Q039	d, e
Q040	a, d, f
Q041	b, d, e, f
Q042	d It is illegal to park on the zigzag lines of a pedestrian crossing for any reason or at any time.
Q043	a, d
Q044	a
Q045	a
Q046	d
Q047	a You need to check for vehicles in your left blind spot.
Q048	b
Q049	b
Q050	a, c, f
Q051	a
Q052	a
Q053	b
Q054	a
Q055	a
Q056	b
Q057	a, b, c
Q058	b, e, f
Q059	a, b
Q060	d
Q061	d

Q062	a All the other actions suggested could be dangerous.
Q063	d
Q064	d
Q065	a
Q066	a You should signal left just as you pass the exit before the one you want to take.
Q067	b
Q068	d
Q069	c
Q070	d This is correct for most roundabouts. Bear in mind that some roundabouts do not have an exit to the left, so the first exit is straight ahead.
Q071	b
Q072	a You often find these on housing estates. Approach with caution and be prepared to give way.
Q073	a, d, e
Q074	b Because the central reserve is narrow, you would partly block the road if you drove to the middle and had to wait.
Q075	d
Q076	d
Q077	c
Q078	a

Answers and explanations

Q079 a

Q080 a, b, c
'd' is wrong because although the double, broken white lines at a junction mean 'give way', you do not necessarily have to stop in order to do so. 'e' is wrong because you may drive on at a pelican crossing when the amber light is flashing if no pedestrians are crossing.

Q081 a, c, e
Note the word 'MUST' in the question, which is asking what the law says.

Q082 a, c, e

Q083 c You should wait for three minutes. If no further train passes you should telephone the signal operator.

Q084 c You are already on the crossing when the warning lights come on, so 'c' is correct.

Q085 b These countdown markers indicate the distance to the stop line at the concealed level crossing.

Q086 c

Q087 d Cyclists are allowed to ride across toucan crossings, unlike other crossings where they must dismount.

Q088 b, d
Toucan crossings are shared by pedestrians and cyclists together.

Q089 b You may drive as soon as the crossing is clear and before the flashing amber light changes to green.

Q090 a

Q091 d It is illegal to reverse from a minor to a major road, so 'a' is wrong. 'b' and 'c' would be dangerous because the road is busy.

Q092 a

Q093 c

Q094 a

Q095 a

Q096 c

Q097 b

Q098 d Always remember to check all round just before steering and give way to any road users.

Q099 d

Theory Test Questions

2001/2002

Road & Traffic Signs

BSM

We won't fail you

Question 1

Mark one answer

You should NOT normally stop on these markings near schools

a except when picking up children

b under any circumstances

c unless there is nowhere else available

d except to set down children

Question 2

Mark one answer

This traffic sign means there is

a a compulsory maximum speed limit

b an advisory maximum speed limit

c a compulsory minimum speed limit

d an advised separation distance

Question 3

Mark one answer

You see this sign at a crossroads. You should

a maintain the same speed

b carry on with great care

c find another route

d telephone the police

Question 4

Mark one answer

You are signalling to turn right in busy traffic. How would you confirm your intention safely?

a Sound the horn

b Give an arm signal

c Flash your headlights

d Position over the centre line

Question 5

Mark one answer

You are on a motorway. Red flashing lights appear above your lane only. What should you do?

a Continue in that lane and look for further information

b Move into another lane in good time

c Pull onto the hard shoulder

d Stop and wait for an instruction to proceed

Question 6

Mark one answer

What does this sign mean?

a Motorcycles only

b No cars

c Cars only

d No motorcycles

Question 7

Mark one answer

You are on a motorway. You see this sign on a lorry that has stopped in the right-hand lane. You should

a move into the right-hand lane

b stop behind the flashing lights

c pass the lorry on the left

d leave the motorway at the next exit

Question 8

Mark one answer

A red traffic light means

a you must stop behind the white stop line

b you may go straight on if there is no other traffic

c you may turn left if it is safe to do so

d you must slow down and prepare to stop if traffic has started to cross

Question 9

Mark one answer

Which arm signal tells you that the car you are following is going to turn left?

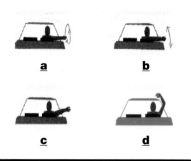

a

b

c

d

Question 10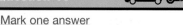

Mark one answer

You must not use your horn when you are stationary

a unless a moving vehicle may cause you danger

b at any time whatsoever

c unless it is used only briefly

d except for signalling that you have just arrived

Question 11

Mark one answer

When drivers flash their headlights at you it means

a that there is a radar speed trap ahead

b that they are giving way to you

c that they are warning you of their presence

d that there is something wrong with your motorcycle

Question 12

Mark one answer

When other drivers flash their headlights at you it means

a that there is a radar speed trap ahead

b that they are giving way to you

c that they are warning you of their presence

d that there is something wrong with your vehicle

Question 13

Mark one answer

You are riding on a motorway. There is a slow-moving vehicle ahead. On the back you see this sign. What should you do?

a Pass on the right

b Pass on the left

c Leave at the next exit

d Drive no further

Question 14

Mark one answer

You MUST obey signs giving orders. These signs are mostly in

a green rectangles

b red triangles

c blue rectangles

d red circles

Question 15

Mark one answer

Traffic signs giving orders are generally which shape?

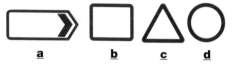

a   b   c   d

Question 16

Mark one answer

Which type of sign tells you NOT to do something?

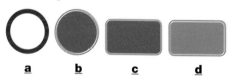

a   b   c   d

Question 17

Mark one answer

What does this sign mean?

a Maximum speed limit with traffic calming

b Minimum speed limit with traffic calming

c '20 cars only' parking zone

d Only 20 cars allowed at any one time

Question 18

Mark one answer

Which sign means no motor vehicles are allowed?

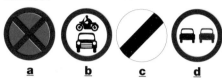

a   b   c   d

Question 19

Mark one answer

Which of these signs means no motor vehicles?

a   b   c   d

Question 20

Mark one answer

What does this sign mean?

a New speed limit 20 mph

b No vehicles over 30 tonnes

c Minimum speed limit 30 mph

d End of 20 mph zone

Question 21

Mark one answer

What does this sign mean?

a No overtaking

b No motor vehicles

c Clearway (no stopping)

d Cars and motorcycles only

Question 23

Mark one answer

What does this sign mean?

a Bend to the right

b Road on the right closed

c No traffic from the right

d No right turn

Question 22

Mark one answer

What does this sign mean?

a No parking

b No road markings

c No through road

d No entry

Question 24

Mark one answer

Which sign means 'no entry'?

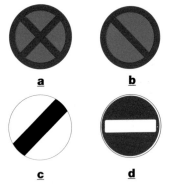

Question 25

Mark one answer

Only

What does this sign mean?

a Route for trams only

b Route for buses only

c Parking for buses only

d Parking for trams only

Question 26

Mark one answer

Which type of vehicle does this sign apply to?

a Wide vehicles

b Long vehicles

c High vehicles

d Heavy vehicles

Question 27

Mark one answer

Which sign means NO motor vehicles allowed?

a   **b**   **c**   **d**

Question 28

Mark one answer

What does this sign mean?

a You have priority

b No motor vehicles

c Two-way traffic

d No overtaking

Question 29

Mark one answer

What does this sign mean?

a Keep in one lane

b Give way to oncoming traffic

c Do not overtake

d Form two lanes

Question 30

Mark one answer

Which sign means no overtaking?

a

b

c

d

Question 31

Mark one answer

What does this sign mean?

a Waiting restrictions apply

b Waiting permitted

c National speed limit applies

d Clearway (no stopping)

Question 32

Mark one answer

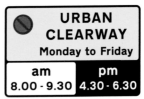

URBAN CLEARWAY Monday to Friday	
am	pm
8.00 - 9.30	4.30 - 6.30

What does this sign mean?

a You can park on the days and times shown

b No parking on the days and times shown

c No parking at all from Monday to Friday

d You can park at any time; the urban clearway ends

Question 33

Mark one answer

Zone ENDS

What does this sign mean?

a End of restricted speed area

b End of restricted parking area

c End of clearway

d End of cycle route

Question 34

Mark one answer

Which sign means 'no stopping'?

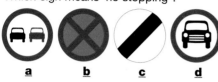

a   **b**   **c**   **d**

Question 35

Mark one answer

What does this sign mean?

a Roundabout

b Crossroads

c No stopping

d No entry

Question 36

Mark one answer

You see this sign ahead. It means

a national speed limit applies

b waiting restrictions apply

c no stopping

d no entry

Question 37

Mark one answer

What does this sign mean?

a Distance to parking place ahead

b Distance to public telephone ahead

c Distance to public house ahead

d Distance to passing place ahead

Question 38

Mark one answer

What does this sign mean?

a Vehicles may not park on the verge or footway

b Vehicles may park on the left-hand side of the road only

c Vehicles may park fully on the verge or footway

d Vehicles may park on the right-hand side of the road only

Question 39

Mark one answer

What does this traffic sign mean?

a No overtaking allowed

b Give priority to oncoming traffic

c Two way traffic

d One-way traffic only

Question 40

Mark one answer

What is the meaning of this traffic sign?

a End of two-way road

b Give priority to vehicles coming towards you

c You have priority over vehicles coming towards you

d Bus lane ahead

Question 41

Mark one answer

Which sign means 'traffic has priority over oncoming vehicles'?

a **b**

c **d**

Question 42

Mark one answer

STOP

What MUST you do when you see this sign?

a Stop, ONLY if traffic is approaching

b Stop, even if the road is clear

c Stop, ONLY if children are waiting to cross

d Stop, ONLY if a red light is showing

Question 43

Mark one answer

What does this sign mean?

a No overtaking

b You are entering a one-way street

c Two-way traffic ahead

d You have priority over vehicles from the opposite direction

Question 45

Mark one answer

At a junction you see this sign partly covered by snow. What does it mean?

a Cross roads

b Give way

c Stop

d Turn right

Question 44

Mark one answer

What shape is a STOP sign at a junction?

a

b

c

d

Question 46

Mark one answer

Which shape is used for a GIVE WAY sign?

a

b

c

d

Question 47

Mark one answer

What does this sign mean?

a Service area 30 miles ahead

b Maximum speed 30 mph

c Minimum speed 30 mph

d Lay-by 30 miles ahead

Question 48

Mark one answer

Which of these signs means turn left ahead?

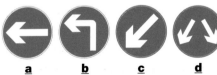

  a   **b**   **c**   **d**

Question 49

Mark one answer

What does this sign mean?

a Buses turning

b Ring road

c Mini roundabout

d Keep right

Question 50

Mark one answer

What does this sign mean?

a Give way to oncoming vehicles

b Approaching traffic passes you on both sides

c Turn off at the next available junction

d Pass either side to get to the same destination

Question 51

Mark one answer

What does this sign mean?

a Route for trams

b Give way to trams

c Route for buses

d Give way to buses

Question 52

Mark one answer

What does a circular traffic sign with a blue background do?

a Give warning of a motorway ahead

b Give directions to a car park

c Give motorway information

d Give an instruction

Question 53

Mark one answer

Which of these signs means that you are entering a one-way street?

a   **b**   **c**   **d**

Question 54

Mark one answer

Where would you see a contraflow bus and cycle lane?

a On a dual carriageway

b On a roundabout

c On an urban motorway

d On a one-way street

Question 55

Mark one answer

What does this sign mean?

a Bus station on the right

b Contraflow bus lane

c With-flow bus lane

d Give way to buses

Question 56

Mark one answer

What does this sign mean?

a With-flow bus and cycle lane

b Contraflow bus and cycle lane

c No buses and cycles allowed

d No waiting for buses and cycles

Question 57

Mark one answer

What does a sign with a brown background show?

a Tourist directions

b Primary roads

c Motorway routes

d Minor routes

Mark one answer

This sign means

a tourist attraction

b beware of trains

c level crossing

d beware of trams

Mark one answer

What are triangular signs for?

a To give warnings

b To give information

c To give orders

d To give directions

Mark one answer

What does this sign mean?

a Turn left ahead

b T-junction

c No through road

d Give way

Mark one answer

What does this sign mean?

a Multi-exit roundabout

b Risk of ice

c Six roads converge

d Place of historical interest

Mark one answer

What does this sign mean?

a Crossroads

b Level crossing with gate

c Level crossing without gate

d Ahead only

Question 63

Mark one answer

What does this sign mean?

a Ring road

b Mini-roundabout

c No vehicles

d Roundabout

Question 64

Mark four answers

Which FOUR of these would be indicated by a triangular road sign?

a Road narrows

b Ahead only

c Low bridge

d Minimum speed

e Children crossing

f T-junction

Question 65

Mark one answer

What does this sign mean?

a Cyclists must dismount

b Cycles are not allowed

c Cycle route ahead

d Cycle in single file

Question 66

Mark one answer

Which sign means that pedestrians may be walking along the road?

a   **b**

c   **d**

Question 67

Mark one answer

Which of these signs warns you of a pedestrian crossing?

a

b

c

d

Question 68

Mark one answer

What does this sign mean?

a No footpath ahead
b Pedestrians only ahead
c Pedestrian crossing ahead
d School crossing ahead

Question 69

Mark one answer

What does this sign mean?

a School crossing patrol
b No pedestrians allowed
c Pedestrian zone — no vehicles
d Pedestrian crossing ahead

Question 70

Mark one answer

Which of these signs means there is a double bend ahead?

a

b

c

d

Question 71

Mark one answer

What does this sign mean?

a Wait at the barriers

b Wait at the crossroads

c Give way to trams

d Give way to farm vehicles

Question 72

Mark one answer

What does this sign mean?

a Humpback bridge

b Humps in the road

c Entrance to tunnel

d Soft verges

Question 73

Mark one answer

What does this sign mean?

a Low bridge ahead

b Tunnel ahead

c Ancient monument ahead

d Accident black spot ahead

Question 74

Mark one answer

What does this sign mean?

a Two-way traffic straight ahead

b Two-way traffic crossing a one-way street

c Two-way traffic over a bridge

d Two-way traffic crosses a two-way road

Question 75

Mark one answer

Which sign means 'two-way traffic crosses a one-way road'?

a

b

c

d

Question 76

Mark one answer

Which of these signs means the end of a dual carriageway?

a

b

c

d

Question 77

Mark one answer

What does this sign mean?

a End of dual carriageway

b Tall bridge

c Road narrows

d End of narrow bridge

Question 78

Mark one answer

What does this sign mean?

a Two-way traffic ahead across a one-way street

b Traffic approaching you has priority

c Two-way traffic straight ahead

d Motorway contraflow system ahead

Mark one answer

What does this sign mean?

a Crosswinds

b Road noise

c Airport

d Adverse camber

Mark one answer

What does this traffic sign mean?

a Slippery road ahead

b Tyres liable to punctures ahead

c Danger ahead

d Service area ahead

Mark one answer

You are about to overtake when you see this sign. You should

a overtake the other driver as quickly as possible

b move to the right to get a better view

c switch your headlights on before overtaking

d hold back until you can see clearly ahead

Mark one answer

What does this sign mean?

a Level crossing with gate or barrier

b Gated road ahead

c Level crossing without gate or barrier

d Cattle grid ahead

Question 83

Mark one answer

What does this sign mean?

a No trams ahead

b Oncoming trams

c Trams crossing ahead

d Trams only

Question 84

Mark one answer

What does this sign mean?

a Adverse camber

b Steep hill downwards

c Uneven road

d Steep hill upwards

Question 85

Mark one answer

What does this sign mean?

a Quayside or river bank

b Steep hill downwards

c Slippery road

d Road liable to flooding

Question 86

Mark one answer

What does this sign mean?

a Uneven road surface

b Bridge over the road

c Road ahead ends

d Water across the road

Question 87

What does this sign mean?

a Humpback bridge
b Traffic calming hump
c Low bridge
d Uneven road

Question 88

Mark one answer

What does this sign mean?

a Turn left for parking area
b No through road on the left
c No entry for traffic turning left
d Turn left for ferry terminal

Question 89

What does this sign mean?

a T-junction
b No through road
c Telephone box ahead
d Toilet ahead

Question 90

Mark one answer

Which sign means 'no through road'?

a   **b**   **c**   **d**

Question 91

Mark one answer

Which of the following signs informs you that you are coming to a No Through Road?

a   **b**   **c**   **d**

Question 92

Mark one answer

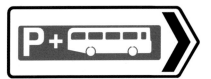

What does this sign mean?

a Direction to park and ride car park

b No parking for buses or coaches

c Directions to bus and coach park

d Parking area for cars and coaches

Question 93

Mark one answer

You are going through a tunnel and you see this sign. What does it mean?

a Direction to emergency pedestrian exit

b Beware of pedestrians, no footpath ahead

c No access for pedestrians

d Beware of pedestrians crossing ahead

Question 94

Mark one answer

Which is the sign for a ring road?

a　　　**b**　　　**c**　　　**d**

Question 95

Mark one answer

What does this sign mean?

a Route for lorries

b Ring road

c Rest area

d Roundabout

Question 96

Mark one answer

What does this sign mean?

a Hilly road

b Humps in road

c Holiday route

d Hospital route

Question 97

Mark one answer

What does this sign mean?

a The right-hand lane ahead is narrow

b Right-hand lane for buses only

c Right-hand lane for turning right

d The right-hand lane is closed

Question 98

Mark one answer

What does this sign mean?

a Change to the left lane

b Leave at the next exit

c Contraflow system

d One-way street

Question 99

Mark three answers

To avoid an accident when entering a contraflow system, you should

a reduce speed in good time

b switch lanes anytime to make progress

c choose an appropriate lane early

d keep the correct separation distance

e increase speed to pass through quickly

f follow other motorists closely to avoid long queues

Question 100

Mark one answer

What does this sign mean?

a Leave motorway at next exit

b Lane for heavy and slow vehicles

c All lorries use the hard shoulder

d Rest area for lorries

Question 101

Mark one answer

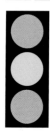

You see this traffic light ahead. Which light(s) will come on next?

a Red alone

b Red and amber together

c Green and amber together

d Green alone

Question 102

Mark one answer

You are approaching a red traffic light. The signal will change from red to

a red and amber, then green

b green, then amber

c amber, then green

d green and amber, then green

Question 103

Mark one answer

A red traffic light means

a you should stop unless turning left

b stop, if you are able to brake safely

c you must stop and wait behind the stop line

d proceed with caution

Question 104

Mark one answer

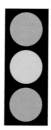

At traffic lights, amber on its own means

a prepare to go

b go if the way is clear

c go if no pedestrians are crossing

d stop at the stop line

Mark one answer

You are approaching traffic lights. Red and amber are showing. This means

a pass the lights if the road is clear

b there is a fault with the lights — take care

c wait for the green light before you pass the lights

d the lights are about to change to red

Mark one answer

You are at a junction controlled by traffic lights. When should you NOT proceed at green?

a When pedestrians are waiting to cross

b When your exit from the junction is blocked

c When you think the lights may be about to change

d When you intend to turn right

Mark one answer

You are in the left-hand lane at traffic lights. You are waiting to turn left. At which of these traffic lights must you NOT move on?

a

b

c

d

Mark one answer

What does this sign mean?

a Traffic lights out of order

b Amber signal out of order

c Temporary traffic lights ahead

d New traffic lights ahead

Question 109

Mark one answer

When traffic lights are out of order, who has priority?

a Traffic going straight on
b Traffic turning right
c Nobody
d Traffic turning left

Question 110

Mark three answers

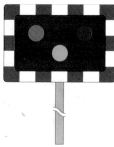

These flashing red lights mean STOP. In which THREE of the following places could you find them?

a Pelican crossings
b Lifting bridges
c Zebra crossings
d Level crossings
e Motorway exits
f Fire stations

Question 111

Mark one answer

What do these zigzag lines at pedestrian crossings mean?

a No parking at any time
b Parking allowed only for a short time
c Slow down to 20 mph
d Sounding horns is not allowed

Question 112

Mark one answer

You are approaching a zebra crossing where pedestrians are waiting. Which arm signal might you give?

a   **b**

c   **d**

Question 113

Mark one answer

The white line along the side of the road
a shows the edge of the carriageway
b shows the approach to a hazard
c means no parking
d means no overtaking

Question 114

Mark one answer

The white line painted in the centre of
the road means
a the area is hazardous and you must
not overtake
b you should give priority to oncoming
vehicles
c do not cross the line unless the road
ahead is clear
d the area is a national speed limit zone

Question 115

Mark one answer

When may you cross a double solid
white line in the middle of the road?
a To pass traffic that is queuing back at
a junction
b To pass a car signalling to turn left
ahead
c To pass a road maintenance vehicle
travelling at 10 mph or less
d To pass a vehicle that is towing a
trailer

Question 116

Mark one answer

A white line like this along the centre of
the road is a
a bus lane marking
b hazard warning
c 'give way' marking
d lane marking

Question 117

Mark one answer

You see this white arrow on the road ahead. It means

a entrance on the left

b all vehicles turn left

c keep left of the hatched markings

d road bending to the left

Question 118

Mark one answer

What does this road marking mean?

a Do not cross the line

b No stopping allowed

c You are approaching a hazard

d No overtaking allowed

Question 119

Mark one answer

This marking appears on the road just before a

a no entry sign

b give way sign

c stop sign

d no through road sign

Question 120

Mark one answer

Where would you see this road marking?

a At traffic lights

b On road humps

c Near a level crossing

d At a box junction

Question 121

Mark one answer

Which is a hazard warning line?

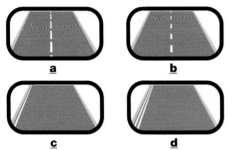

a

b

c

d

Question 122

Mark one answer

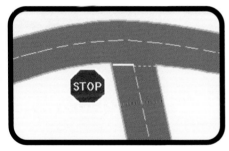

At this junction there is a stop sign with a solid white line on the road surface.
Why is there a stop sign here?

a Speed on the major road is de-restricted

b It is a busy junction

c Visibility along the major road is restricted

d There are hazard warning lines in the centre of the road

Question 123

Mark one answer

You see this line across the road at the entrance to a roundabout. What does it mean?

a Give way to traffic from the right

b Traffic from the left has right of way

c You have right of way

d Stop at the line

Question 124

Mark one answer

Where would you find this road marking?

a At a railway crossing

b At a junction

c On a motorway

d On a pedestrian crossing

Question 125

Mark <u>one</u> <u>answer</u>

How will a police officer in a patrol vehicle normally get you to stop?

a Flash the headlights, indicate left and point to the left

b Wait until you stop, then approach you

c Use the siren, overtake, cut in front and stop

d Pull alongside you, use the siren and wave you to stop

Question 126

Mark <u>one</u> <u>answer</u>

There is a police car following you. The police officer flashes the headlights and points to the left. What should you do?

a Turn at the next left

b Pull up on the left

c Stop immediately

d Move over to the left

Question 127

Mark <u>one</u> <u>answer</u>

You approach a junction. The traffic lights are not working. A police officer gives this signal. You should

a turn left only

b turn right only

c stop level with the officer's arm

d stop at the stop line

Question 128

Mark <u>one</u> <u>answer</u>

How should you give an arm signal to turn left?

a

b

c

d

Question 129

Mark one answer

The driver of the car in front is giving this arm signal. What does it mean?

a The driver is slowing down
b The driver intends to turn right
c The driver wishes to overtake
d The driver intends to turn left

Question 130

Mark one answer

Your indicators are difficult to see due to bright sunshine. When using them you should

a also give an arm signal
b sound your horn
c flash your headlamp
d keep both hands on the handlebars

Question 131

Mark one answer

The driver of this car is giving an arm signal. What are they about to do?

a Turn to the right
b Turn to the left
c Go straight ahead
d Let pedestrians cross

Question 132

Mark one answer

You are giving an arm signal ready to turn left. Why should you NOT continue with the arm signal while you turn?

a Because you might hit a pedestrian on the corner
b Because you will have less steering control
c Because you will need to keep the clutch applied
d Because other motorists will think that you are stopping on the corner

Question 133

Mark one answer

How should you give an arm signal to turn left?

a

b

c

d

Question 134

Mark one answer

When may you sound the horn?

a To give you right of way

b To attract a friend's attention

c To warn others of your presence

d To make slower drivers move over

Question 135

Mark one answer

Why should you make sure that you have cancelled your indicators after turning?

a To avoid flattening the battery

b To avoid misleading other road users

c To avoid dazzling other road users

d To avoid damage to the indicator relay

Question 136

Mark one answer

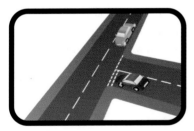

You are waiting at a T-junction. A vehicle is coming from the right with the left signal flashing. What should you do?

a Move out and accelerate hard

b Wait until the vehicle starts to turn in

c Pull out before the vehicle reaches the junction

d Move out slowly

Question 137

Mark one answer

When may you use hazard warning lights when driving?

a Instead of sounding the horn in a built-up area between 11.30 pm and 7 am

b On a motorway or unrestricted dual carriageway, to warn of a hazard ahead

c On rural routes, after a warning sign of animals

d On the approach to toucan crossings where cyclists are waiting to cross

Question 138

Mark one answer

Where would you see these road markings?

a At a level crossing

b On a motorway slip road

c At a pedestrian crossing

d On a single-track road

Question 139

Mark one answer

When may you NOT overtake on the left?

a On a free-flowing motorway or dual carriageway

b When the traffic is moving slowly in queues

c On a one-way street

d When the car in front is signalling to turn right

Question 140

Mark one answer

You are driving on a motorway. There is a slow-moving vehicle ahead. On the back you see this sign. You should

a pass on the right

b pass on the left

c leave at the next exit

d drive no further

Question 141

Mark one answer

What does this motorway sign mean?

a Change to the lane on your left

b Leave the motorway at the next exit

c Change to the opposite carriageway

d Pull up on the hard shoulder

Question 142

Mark one answer

What does this motorway sign mean?

a Temporary minimum speed 50 mph

b No services for 50 miles

c Obstruction 50 metres (164 feet) ahead

d Temporary maximum speed 50 mph

Question 143

Mark one answer

What does this sign mean?

a Through traffic to use left lane

b Right-hand lane T-junction only

c Right-hand lane closed ahead

d 11 tonne weight limit

Question 144

Mark one answer

On a motorway this sign means
a move over onto the hard shoulder
b overtaking on the left only
c leave the motorway at the next exit
d move to the lane on your left

Question 145

Mark one answer

Nottingham
A46

25

What does '25' mean on this motorway sign?
a The distance to the nearest town
b The route number of the road
c The number of the next junction
d The speed limit on the slip road

Question 146

Mark one answer
The right-hand lane of a three-lane motorway is
a for lorries only
b an overtaking lane
c the right-turn lane
d an acceleration lane

Question 147

Mark one answer
Where can you find reflective amber studs on a motorway?
a Separating the slip road from the motorway
b On the left-hand edge of the road
c On the right-hand edge of the road
d Separating the lanes

Question 148

Mark one answer
Where on a motorway would you find green reflective studs?
a Separating driving lanes
b Between the hard shoulder and the carriageway
c At slip road entrances and exits
d Between the carriageway and the central reservation

Question 149

Mark one answer

You are travelling along a motorway. You see this sign. You should

a leave the motorway at the next exit

b turn left immediately

c change lane

d move onto the hard shoulder

Question 150

Mark one answer

You see these signs overhead on the motorway. They mean

a leave the motorway at the next exit

b all vehicles use the hard shoulder

c sharp bend to the left ahead

d stop, all lanes ahead closed

Question 151

Mark one answer

This sign is of particular importance to motorcyclists. It means

a side winds

b airport

c slippery road

d service area

Question 152

Mark one answer

What does this sign mean?

a No motor vehicles

b End of motorway

c No through road

d End of bus lane

Question 153

Mark one answer

Which of these signs means that the national speed limit applies?

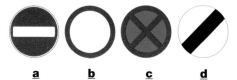

a　**b**　**c**　**d**

Question 154

Mark one answer

What is the maximum speed on a single carriageway road?

a 50 mph
b 60 mph
c 40 mph
d 70 mph

Question 155

Mark one answer

What does this sign mean?

a End of motorway
b End of restriction
c Lane ends ahead
d Free recovery ends

Question 156

Mark one answer

Which one of these signs are you allowed to ride past on a solo motorcycle?

a   **b**   **c**   **d**

Question 157

Mark one answer

This sign is advising you to

a follow the route diversion
b follow the signs to the picnic area
c give way to pedestrians
d give way to cyclists

Question 158

Mark one answer

Which of these signals should you give when slowing or stopping your motorcycle?

a   **b**

c   **d**

Question 159

<u>Mark</u> <u>one</u> <u>answer</u>

Why would this temporary speed limit sign be shown?

a To warn of the end of the motorway

b To warn you of a low bridge

c To warn you of a junction ahead

d To warn of road works ahead

Answers and explanations

Q001   b
Q002   a
Q003   b
Q004   b
Q005   b
Q006   d
Q007   c
Q008   a
Q009   a
Q010   a
Q011   c
Q012   c 'c' is the correct answer because that is what flashing your headlights is supposed to mean. Not everyone knows or obeys the rules and may flash their headlights for other reasons, so always try to make sure what they mean before you decide on any action.
Q013   b
Q014   d
Q015   d
Q016   a Red circles tell you what you must not do. Rectangles usually give you information.
Q017   a
Q018   b
Q019   a
Q020   d

Q021   b
Q022   d
Q023   d
Q024   d
Q025   a
Q026   c
Q027   b
Q028   d
Q029   c
Q030   b
Q031   a There will also be a plate indicating when the restriction applies.
Q032   b
Q033   b
Q034   b
Q035   c
Q036   c This is a clearway sign and you must not stop at all.
Q037   a
Q038   c
Q039   b
Q040   c
Q041   c
Q042   b You must always stop at a stop sign.
Q043   d
Q044   d
Q045   c
Q046   d
Q047   c

Answers and explanations

Q048	b		Q076	d
Q049	c		Q077	a
Q050	d		Q078	c
Q051	a		Q079	a
Q052	d Circular signs with blue backgrounds tell you what you must do.		Q080	c
			Q081	d It is dangerous to overtake when you see this sign because the dip in the road could be hiding oncoming traffic.
Q053	b			
Q054	d			
Q055	b			
Q056	a		Q082	a
Q057	a		Q083	c
Q058	a		Q084	b
Q059	a		Q085	a
Q060	b		Q086	d
Q061	b		Q087	a
Q062	a		Q088	b
Q063	d		Q089	b
Q064	a, c, e, f		Q090	c
Q065	c		Q091	c
Q066	a		Q092	a
Q067	a		Q093	a
Q068	c		Q094	c
Q069	d		Q095	b
Q070	b		Q096	c
Q071	c		Q097	d
Q072	b		Q098	c
Q073	b Red triangles usually give a warning.		Q099	a, c, d
			Q100	b
Q074	b		Q101	a
Q075	b			

Answers and explanations

Q102 a The sequence of traffic lights is red, then red and amber, then green, then amber alone, then red.

Q103 c You must always stop at a red traffic light.

Q104 d An amber light means stop, and the lights will next change to red.

Q105 c The next light will be green and you must wait to drive on until it appears.

Q106 b

Q107 a

Q108 a

Q109 c

Q110 b, d, f

Q111 a

Q112 a

Q113 a

Q114 c

Q115 c

Q116 b

Q117 c

Q118 c

Q119 b

Q120 b

Q121 a Long lines with short gaps between them in the middle of the road are hazard warning lines. The more paint the more danger.

Q122 c Because the major road is on a bend, your vision is restricted to both left and right.

Q123 a

Q124 b

Q125 a

Q126 b You must stop, but 'c' is wrong because it may not be safe to stop immediately.

Q127 d

Q128 c

Q129 d

Q130 a

Q131 b

Q132 b

Q133 c

Q134 c Sounding your horn has the same meaning as flashing your headlights – to warn of your presence.

Q135 b

Answers and explanations

Q136 b The approaching vehicle might have left the signal on by mistake, or intended to stop after the junction. Always wait long enough to be sure the vehicle is really turning left.

Q137 b Note that the question states 'when driving'. The types of roads in 'b' are the only places where it is legal to use hazard warning lights while your car is moving.

Q138 b

Q139 a You must not overtake on the left on a motorway or dual carriageway unless you are moving in queues of slow-moving traffic.

Q140 b

Q141 a Obviously you must make sure it is safe before doing so.

Q142 d

Q143 c Always look well ahead and you will have plenty of time to react.

Q144 d You must go no further in that lane. You may change lanes and proceed, unless flashing red lights appear above all of them.

Q145 c
Q146 b
Q147 c
Q148 c
Q149 a
Q150 a
Q151 a
Q152 b
Q153 d
Q154 b
Q155 b
Q156 d
Q157 a
Q158 a
Q159 d

Theory
Test
Questions

2001/2002

Documents

Question 1

Mark one answer

A police officer asks to see your documents. You do not have them with you. You may produce them at a police station within

a 5 days
b 7 days
c 14 days
d 21 days

Question 2

Mark four answers

You have passed CBT (Compulsory Basic Training). You want a Direct Access test. You must

a be aged 21 or over
b not exceed 60 mph
c have an approved instructor with you
d remain in radio contact while learning
e only learn in daylight hours
f wear fluorescent or reflective clothing

Question 3

Mark two answers

Which TWO of these are NOT required to have an MOT certificate?

a Motorcycle
b Small trailer
c Ambulance
d Caravan

Question 4

Mark three answers

What should you bring with you when taking your practical motorcycle test?

a A service record book
b An insurance certificate
c A signed driving licence
d An MOT certificate
e A CBT (Compulsory Basic Training) certificate
f Signed photo identity

Question 5

Mark one answer

What is the legal minimum insurance cover you must have to drive on public roads?

a Third party, fire and theft
b Fully comprehensive
c Third party only
d Personal injury cover

Question 6

Mark one answer

Compulsory Basic Training (CBT) can only be carried out by

a any ADI (Approved Driving Instructor)
b any road safety officer
c any DSA (Driving Standards Agency) approved training body
d any motorcycle main dealer

Question 7

Mark three answers

You have third party insurance.
What does this cover?

Damage to your own vehicle

Damage to your vehicle by fire

Injury to another person

Damage to someone's property

Damage to other vehicles

Injury to yourself

Question 8

Mark one answer

Before taking a motorcycle test you need

a full moped licence

a full car licence

a CBT (Compulsory Basic Training)
certificate

12 months' riding experience

Question 9

Mark two answers

For which TWO of these must you show
your motor insurance certificate?

When you are taking your driving test

When buying or selling a vehicle

When a police officer asks you for it

When you are taxing your vehicle

When having an MOT inspection

Question 10

Mark one answer

Vehicle excise duty is often called
'Road Tax' or 'The Tax Disc'. You must

a keep it with your registration
document

b display it clearly on your vehicle

c keep it concealed safely in your
vehicle

d carry it on you at all times

Question 11

Mark one answer

Motor cars must FIRST have an MOT
test certificate when they are

a one year old

b three years old

c five years old

d seven years old

Question 12

Mark one answer

Before riding anyone else's motorcycle
you should make sure that

a the owner has third party insurance
cover

b your own motorcycle has insurance
cover

c the motorcycle is insured for your use

d the owner has the insurance
documents with them

Question 13

Mark one answer

Your vehicle needs a current MOT certificate. You do not have one. Until you do have one you will not be able to renew your

a driving licence

b vehicle insurance

c road tax disc

d vehicle registration document

Question 14

Mark two answers

For which TWO of these must you show your motorcycle insurance certificate?

a When you are taking your practical test

b When buying or selling a motorcycle

c When a police officer asks you for it

d When you are taxing your motorcycle

e When having an MOT inspection

Question 15

Mark three answers

Which THREE of the following do you need before you can drive legally?

a A valid driving licence with signature

b A valid tax disc displayed on your vehicle

c Proof of your identity

d Proper insurance cover

e Breakdown cover

f A vehicle handbook

Question 16

Mark one answer

Vehicle excise duty is often called 'Road Tax' or 'The Tax Disc'. You must

a keep it with your registration document

b display it clearly on your motorcycle

c keep it concealed safely in your motorcycle

d carry it on you at all times

Question 17

Mark three answers

Which THREE pieces of information are found on a vehicle registration document?

a Registered keeper

b Make of the vehicle

c Service history details

d Date of the MOT

e Type of insurance cover

f Engine size

Question 18

Mark one answer

Motorcycles must FIRST have an MOT test certificate when they are

a one year old

b three years old

c five years old

d seven years old

Question 19

Mark three answers

You have a duty to contact the licensing authority when

a you go abroad on holiday
b you change your vehicle
c you change your name
d your job status is changed
e your permanent address changes
f your job involves travelling abroad

Question 20

Mark one answer

Your motorcycle needs a current MOT certificate. You do not have one. Until you do have one you will not be able to renew your

a driving licence
b motorcycle insurance
c road tax disc
d motorcycle registration document

Question 21

Mark three answers

You must notify the licensing authority when

a your health affects your driving
b your eyesight does not meet a set standard
c you intend lending your vehicle
d your vehicle requires an MOT certificate
e you change your vehicle

Question 22

Mark three answers

Which THREE of the following do you need before you can ride legally?

a A valid driving licence with signature
b A valid tax disc displayed on your motorcycle
c Proof of your identity
d Proper insurance cover
e Breakdown cover
f A vehicle handbook

Question 23

Mark one answer

You have just bought a secondhand vehicle. When should you tell the licensing authority of change of ownership?

a Immediately
b After 28 days
c When an MOT is due
d Only when you insure it

Question 24

Mark three answers

Which THREE pieces of information are found on a registration document?

a Registered keeper
b Make of the motorcycle
c Service history details
d Date of the MOT
e Type of insurance cover
f Engine size

Question 25

Mark two answers

Your vehicle is insured third party only. This covers

a damage to your vehicle
b damage to other vehicles
c injury to yourself
d injury to others
e all damage and injury

Question 26

Mark three answers

You have a duty to contact the licensing authority when

a you go abroad on holiday
b you change your motorcycle
c you change your name
d your job status is changed
e your permanent address changes
f your job involves travelling abroad

Question 27

Mark one answer

Your motor insurance policy has an excess of £100. What does this mean?

a The insurance company will pay the first £100 of any claim
b You will be paid £100 if you do not have an accident
c Your vehicle is insured for a value of £100 if it is stolen
d You will have to pay the first £100 of any claim

Question 28

Mark three answers

You must notify the licensing authority when

a your health affects your riding
b your eyesight does not meet a set standard
c you intend lending your motorcycle
d your motorcycle requires an MOT certificate
e you change your motorcycle

Question 29

Mark two answers

You have just passed your practical driving test. Within two years you get six penalty points on your licence. You will have to

a retake only your theory test
b retake your theory and practical tests
c retake only your practical test
d re-apply for your full licence immediately
e re-apply for your provisional licence

Question 30

Mark one answer

You have just bought a secondhand motorcycle. When should you tell the licensing authority of change of ownership?

a Immediately
b After 28 days
c When an MOT is due
d Only when you insure it

Question 31

Mark one answer

When you apply to renew your vehicle excise licence (tax disc) you must produce

a a valid insurance certificate

b the old tax disc

c the vehicle handbook

d a valid driving licence

Question 32

Mark two answers

Your motorcycle is insured third party only. This covers

a damage to your motorcycle

b damage to other vehicles

c injury to yourself

d injury to others

e all damage and injury

Question 33

Mark one answer

What is the legal minimum insurance cover you must have to drive on public roads?

a Fire and theft

b Theft only

c Third party

d Fire only

Question 34

Mark one answer

Your motorcycle insurance policy has an excess of £100. What does this mean?

a The insurance company will pay the first £100 of any claim

b You will be paid £100 if you do not have an accident

c Your motorcycle is insured for a value of £100 if it is stolen

d You will have to pay the first £100 of any claim

Question 35

Mark one answer

To drive on the road learners MUST

a have NO penalty points on their licence

b have taken professional instruction

c have a signed, valid provisional licence

d apply for a driving test within 12 months

Question 36

Mark two answers

You have just passed your practical motorcycle test. Within two years you get six penalty points on your licence. You will have to

a retake only your theory test

b retake your theory and practical tests

c retake only your practical test

d re-apply for your full licence immediately

e re-apply for your provisional licence

Question 37

Mark two answers

To supervise a learner driver you must

a have held a full licence for at least 3 years

b be at least 21

c be an approved driving instructor

d hold an advanced driving certificate

Question 38

Mark one answer

When you apply to renew your motorcycle excise licence (tax disc) you must produce

a a valid insurance certificate

b the old tax disc

c the motorcycle handbook

d a valid driving licence

Question 39

Mark one answer

Before driving anyone else's motor vehicle you should make sure that

a the vehicle owner has third party insurance cover

b your own vehicle has insurance cover

c the vehicle is insured for your use

d the owner has left the insurance documents in the vehicle

Question 40

Mark one answer

What is the legal minimum insurance cover you must have to ride on public roads?

a Fire and theft

b Theft only

c Third party

d Fire only

Question 41

Mark one answer

The cost of your insurance may be reduced if

a your car is large and powerful

b you are using the car for work purposes

c you have penalty points on your licence

d you are over 25 years old

Question 42

Mark one answer

What is the legal minimum insurance cover you must have to ride on public roads?

a Third party, fire and theft

b Fully comprehensive

c Third party only

d Personal injury cover

Question 43

Mark one answer

An MOT certificate is normally valid for

a three years after the date it was issued

b 10,000 miles

c one year after the date it was issued

d 30,000 miles

Question 44

Mark one answer

You want a licence to ride a large motorcycle via direct access. You will

a not require L plates if you have passed a car test

b require L plates only when learning on your own machine

c require L plates while learning with a qualified instructor

d not require L plates if you have passed a moped test

Question 45

Mark one answer

Your car needs an MOT certificate. If you drive without one this could invalidate your

a vehicle service record

b insurance

c road tax disc

d vehicle registration document

Question 46

Mark one answer

You are a learner motorcyclist. The law states that you can carry a passenger when

a your motorcycle is no larger than 125cc

b your pillion passenger is a full licence-holder

c you have passed your test for a full licence

d you have had three years' experience of riding

Question 47

Mark one answer

When is it legal to drive a car over three years old without an MOT certificate?

a Up to seven days after the old certificate has run out

b When driving to an MOT centre to arrange an appointment

c Just after buying a secondhand car with no MOT

d When driving to an appointment at an MOT centre

Question 48

Mark one answer

After passing your motorcycle test you must exchange the pass certificate for a full motorcycle licence within

a six months

b one year

c two years

d five years

Question 49

Mark one answer

A cover note is a document issued before you receive your

a driving licence

b insurance certificate

c registration document

d MOT certificate

Question 50

Mark two answers

For which TWO of these must you show your motorcycle insurance certificate?

a When you are taking your motorcycle test

b When buying or selling a machine

c When a police officer asks you for it

d When you are taxing your machine

e When having an MOT inspection

Question 51

Mark two answers

The cost of your insurance may be reduced if you

a are over 25 years old

b are under 25 years old

c do not wear glasses

d pass the driving test first time

e complete the Pass Plus scheme

Question 52

Mark one answer

How old must you be to supervise a learner driver?

a 18 years old

b 19 years old

c 20 years old

d 21 years old

Question 53

Mark one answer

When you buy a motorcycle you will need a vehicle registration document from

a any MOT testing station

b the person selling the motorcycle

c your local council offices

d your local trading standards officer

Question 54

Mark one answer

A newly-qualified driver must

a display green 'L' plates
b not exceed 40 mph for 12 months
c be accompanied on a motorway
d have valid motor insurance

Question 55

Mark three answers

You hold a provisional motorcycle licence. This means you must NOT

a exceed 30 mph
b ride on a motorway
c ride after dark
d carry a pillion passenger
e ride without 'L' plates displayed

Question 56

Mark three answers

Which of the following information is found on your motorcycle registration document?

a Make and model
b Service history record
c Ignition key security number
d Engine size and number
e Purchase price
f Year of first registration

Question 57

Mark one answer

A theory test pass certificate will not be valid after

a 6 months
b 1 year
c 18 months
d 2 years

Question 58

Mark one answer

A theory test pass certificate is valid for

a two years
b three years
c four years
d five years

Question 59

Mark one answer

A full category A1 licence will allow you to ride a motorcycle up to

a 125cc
b 250cc
c 350cc
d 425cc

Answers and explanations

Q001 b You may select the police station of your choice.

Q002 a, c, d, f

Q003 b, d

Q004 c, e, f

Q005 c This only covers damage to other people and their property.

Q006 c

Q007 c, d, e

Q008 c

Q009 c, d

Q010 b

Q011 b

Q012 c Your own motorbike insurance is very unlikely to cover you to drive another person's motorbike.

Q013 c When you renew your road tax disc you must produce a valid certificate of insurance and also a current MOT certificate if your car is over three years old.

Q014 c, d

Q015 a, b, d

Q016 b

Q017 a, b, f

Q018 b

Q019 b, c, e

Q020 c

Q021 a, b, e

Q022 a, b, d

Q023 a

Q024 a, b, f

Q025 b, d

Q026 b, c, e

Q027 d Agreeing to pay an excess may enable you to obtain a lower premium.

Q028 a, b, e

Q029 b, e

Q030 a

Q031 a

Q032 b, d

Q033 c

Q034 d

Q035 c You are not allowed to drive until you have applied for and received your provisional licence and have signed it in ink

Q036 b, e

Q037 a, b

Q038 a

Q039 c Your own vehicle insurance may cover you as a passenger in another person's vehicle but very rarely covers you to drive it.

Q040 c

Answers and explanations

Q041 **d** Drivers over 25 years old have less accidents than younger drivers. As they make fewer insurance claims, the cost of their premiums is usually less.

Q042 c

Q043 c

Q044 c

Q045 b

Q046 c

Q047 **d** If your motorcycle is over three years old and has no valid MOT certificate, you must pre-book an appointment at an MOT centre before you drive it there.

Q048 c

Q049 b

Q050 c, d

Q051 a, e

Q052 d

Q053 b

Q054 d

Q055 b, d, e

Q056 a, d, f

Q057 d

Q058 a

Q059 a

Theory Test Questions

2001/2002

Accidents

We won't fail you

Question 1

Mark <u>one</u> answer

When are you allowed to use hazard warning lights?

a When stopped and temporarily obstructing traffic

b When travelling during darkness without headlights

c When parked for shopping on double yellow lines

d When travelling slowly because you are lost

Question 2

Mark <u>one</u> answer

You are riding on a motorway. The car in front switches on its hazard warning lights whilst moving. This means

a they are going to take the next exit

b there is a danger ahead

c there is a police car in the left lane

d they are trying to change lanes

Question 3

Mark <u>one</u> answer

You are on the motorway. Luggage falls from your vehicle. What should you do?

a Stop at the next emergency telephone and contact the police

b Stop on the motorway and put on hazard lights while you pick it up

c Walk back up the motorway to pick it up

d Pull up on the hard shoulder and wave traffic down

Question 4

Mark <u>one</u> answer

You are on a motorway. A large box falls onto the road from a lorry. The lorry does not stop. You should

a go to the next emergency telephone and inform the police

b catch up with the lorry and try to get the driver's attention

c stop close to the box until the police arrive

d pull over to the hard shoulder, then remove the box

Question 5

Mark <u>two</u> answers

You are on a motorway. When can you use hazard warning lights?

a When a vehicle is following too closely

b When you slow down quickly because of danger ahead

c When you are towing another vehicle

d When driving on the hard shoulder

e When you have broken down on the hard shoulder

Question 6

Mark two answers

For which TWO should you use hazard warning lights?

a When you slow down quickly on a motorway because of a hazard ahead

b When you have broken down

c When you wish to stop on double yellow lines

d When you need to park on the pavement

Question 7

Mark one answer

You are on the motorway. Luggage falls from your motorcycle. What should you do?

a Stop at the next emergency telephone and contact the police

b Stop on the motorway and put on hazard lights whilst you pick it up

c Walk back up the motorway to pick it up

d Pull up on the hard shoulder and wave traffic down

Question 8

Mark three answers

You have broken down on a motorway. When you use the emergency telephone you will be asked

a for the number on the telephone that you are using

b for your driving licence details

c for the name of your vehicle insurance company

d for details of yourself and your vehicle

e whether you belong to a motoring organisation

Question 9

Mark four answers

You are involved in an accident with another vehicle. Someone is injured. Your motorcycle is damaged. Which FOUR of the following should you find out?

a Whether the driver owns the other vehicle involved

b The other driver's name, address and telephone number

c The make and registration number of the other vehicle

d The occupation of the other driver

e The details of the other driver's vehicle insurance

f Whether the other driver is licensed to drive

Question 10

Mark three answers

Which of these items should you carry in your vehicle for use in the event of an accident?

a Road map
b Can of petrol
c Jump leads
d Fire extinguisher
e First Aid kit
f Warning triangle

Question 11

Mark three answers

You have broken down on a motorway. When you use the emergency telephone you will be asked

a for the number on the telephone that you are using
b for your driving licence details
c for the name of your vehicle insurance company
d for details of yourself and your motorcycle
e whether you belong to a motoring organisation

Question 12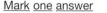

Mark one answer

At the scene of an accident you should

a not put yourself at risk
b go to those casualties who are screaming
c pull everybody out of their vehicles
d leave vehicle engines switched on

Question 13

Mark one answer

You are on a motorway. When can you use hazard warning lights?

a When a vehicle is following too closely
b When you slow down quickly because of danger ahead
c When you are being towed by another vehicle
d When riding on the hard shoulder

Question 14

Mark four answers

You are the first to arrive at the scene of an accident. Which FOUR of these should you do?

a Leave as soon as another motorist arrives
b Switch off the vehicle engine(s)
c Move uninjured people away from the vehicle(s)
d Call the emergency services
e Warn other traffic

Question 15

Mark one answer

You are involved in an accident. How can you reduce the risk of fire to your motorcycle?

a Keep the engine running

b Open the choke

c Turn the fuel tap to reserve

d Use the engine cut out switch

Question 16

Mark one answer

An accident has just happened. An injured person is lying in the busy road. What is the FIRST thing you should do to help?

a Treat the person for shock

b Warn other traffic

c Place them in the recovery position

d Make sure the injured person is kept warm

Question 17

Mark three answers

You are the first person to arrive at an accident where people are badly injured. Which THREE should you do?

a Switch on your own hazard warning lights

b Make sure that someone telephones for an ambulance

c Try and get people who are injured to drink something

d Move the people who are injured clear of their vehicles

e Get people who are not injured clear of the scene

Question 18

Mark one answer

You arrive at the scene of a motorcycle accident. The rider is injured. When should the helmet be removed?

a Only when it is essential

b Always straight away

c Only when the motorcyclist asks

d Always, unless they are in shock

Question 19

Mark three answers

You arrive at a serious motorcycle accident. The motorcyclist is unconscious and bleeding. Your main priorities should be to

a try to stop the bleeding

b make a list of witnesses

c check the casualty's breathing

d take the numbers of the vehicles involved

e sweep up any loose debris

f check the casualty's airways

Question 20

Mark one answer

You arrive at an accident. A motorcyclist is unconscious. Your FIRST priority is the casualty's

a breathing

b bleeding

c broken bones

d bruising

Question 21

Mark three answers

At an accident a casualty is unconscious. Which THREE of the following should you check urgently?

a Circulation

b Airway

c Shock

d Breathing

e Broken bones

Question 22

Mark three answers

You arrive at the scene of an accident. It has just happened and someone is unconscious. Which of the following should be given urgent priority to help them?

a Clear the airway and keep it open

b Try to get them to drink water

c Check that they are breathing

d Look for any witnesses

e Stop any heavy bleeding

f Take the numbers of vehicles involved

Question 23

Mark three answers

At an accident someone is unconscious. Your main priorities should be to

a sweep up the broken glass

b take the names of witnesses

c count the number of vehicles involved

d check the airway is clear

e make sure they are breathing

f stop any heavy bleeding

Question 24

Mark three answers

You have stopped at the scene of an accident to give help. Which THREE things should you do?

a Keep injured people warm and comfortable

b Keep injured people calm by talking to them reassuringly

c Keep injured people on the move by walking them around

d Give injured people a warm drink

e Make sure that injured people are not left alone

Question 25

Mark three answers

You arrive at the scene of an accident. It has just happened and someone is injured. Which THREE of the following should be given urgent priority?

a Stop any severe bleeding

b Get them a warm drink

c Check that their breathing is OK

d Take numbers of vehicles involved

e Look for witnesses

f Clear their airway and keep it open

Question 26

Mark two answers

At an accident a casualty has stopped breathing. You should

a remove anything that is blocking the mouth

b keep the head tilted forwards as far as possible

c raise the legs to help with circulation

d try to give the casualty something to drink

e keep the head tilted back as far as possible

Question 27

Mark four answers

You are at the scene of an accident. Someone is suffering from shock. You should

a reassure them constantly

b offer them a cigarette

c keep them warm

d avoid moving them if possible

e loosen any tight clothing

f give them a warm drink

Question 28

Mark one answer

Which of the following should you NOT do at the scene of an accident?

a Warn other traffic by switching on your hazard warning lights

b Call the emergency services immediately

c Offer someone a cigarette to calm them down

d Ask drivers to switch off their engines

Question 29

Mark two answers

There has been an accident. The driver is suffering from shock. You should

a give them a drink

b reassure them

c not leave them alone

d offer them a cigarette

e ask who caused the accident

Question 30

Mark three answers

You are at the scene of an accident. Someone is suffering from shock. You should

a offer them a cigarette

b offer them a warm drink

c keep them warm

d loosen any tight clothing

e reassure them constantly

Question 31

Mark one answer

You have to treat someone for shock at the scene of an accident. You should

a reassure them constantly

b walk them around to calm them down

c give them something cold to drink

d cool them down as soon as possible

Question 32

Mark one answer

You arrive at the scene of a motorcycle accident. No other vehicle is involved. The rider is unconscious, lying in the middle of the road. The first thing you should do is

a move the rider out of the road

b warn other traffic

c clear the road of debris

d give the rider reassurance

Question 33

Mark one answer

At an accident a small child is not breathing. When giving mouth to mouth you should breathe

a sharply

b gently

c heavily

d rapidly

Question 34

Mark three answers

To start mouth to mouth on a casualty you should

a tilt their head forward

b clear the airway

c turn them on their side

d tilt their head back

e pinch the nostrils together

f put their arms across their chest

Question 35

Mark one answer

When you are giving mouth to mouth you should only stop when

a you think the casualty is dead

b the casualty can breathe without help

c the casualty has turned blue

d you think the ambulance is coming

Question 36

Mark one answer

You arrive at the scene of an accident. There has been an engine fire and someone's hands and arms have been burnt. You should NOT

a douse the burn thoroughly with cool liquid

b lay the casualty down

c remove anything sticking to the burn

d reassure them constantly

Question 37

Mark one answer

You arrive at an accident where someone is suffering from severe burns. You should

a apply lotions to the injury

b burst any blisters

c remove anything stuck to the burns

d douse the burns with cool liquid

Question 38

Mark one answer

You arrive at an accident where someone is suffering from severe burns. You should

a burst any blisters

b douse the burns thoroughly with cool liquid

c apply lotions to the injury

d remove anything sticking to the burns

Question 39

Mark two answers

You arrive at the scene of an accident. A pedestrian has a severe bleeding wound on their leg, although it is not broken. What should you do?

a Dab the wound to stop bleeding

b Keep both legs flat on the ground

c Apply firm pressure to the wound

d Raise the leg to lessen bleeding

e Fetch them a warm drink

Question 40

Mark one answer

You arrive at the scene of an accident. A passenger is bleeding badly from an arm wound. What should you do?

a Apply pressure over the wound and keep the arm down

b Dab the wound

c Get them a drink

d Apply pressure over the wound and raise the arm

Question 41

Mark one answer

You arrive at the scene of an accident. A pedestrian is bleeding heavily from a leg wound but the leg is not broken. What should you do?

a Dab the wound to stop the bleeding

b Keep both legs flat on the ground

c Apply firm pressure to the wound

d Fetch them a warm drink

Question 42

Mark one answer

At an accident a casualty is unconscious but still breathing. You should only move them if

a an ambulance is on its way

b bystanders advise you to

c there is further danger

d bystanders will help you to

Question 43

Mark one answer

At an accident you suspect a casualty has back injuries. The area is safe. You should

a offer them a drink

b not move them

c raise their legs

d offer them a cigarette

Question 44

Mark one answer

At an accident it is important to look after the casualty. When the area is safe, you should

a get them out of the vehicle

b give them a drink

c give them something to eat

d keep them in the vehicle

Question 45

Mark one answer

A tanker is involved in an accident. Which sign would show that the tanker is carrying dangerous goods?

a

b

c

d

Question 46

Mark one answer

While driving, a warning light on your vehicle's instrument panel comes on. You should

a continue if the engine sounds alright

b hope that it is just a temporary electrical fault

c deal with the problem when there is more time

d check out the problem quickly and safely

Question 47

Mark three answers

For which THREE should you use your hazard warning lights?

a When you are parking in a restricted area

b When you are temporarily obstructing traffic

c To warn following traffic of a hazard ahead

d When you have broken down

e When only stopping for a short time

Question 48

Mark one answer

You have broken down on a two-way road. You have a warning triangle. You should place the warning triangle at least how far from your vehicle?

a 5 metres (16 feet)

b 25 metres (82 feet)

c 45 metres (147 feet)

d 100 metres (328 feet)

Question 49

Mark one answer

You are in an accident on a two-way road. You have a warning triangle with you. At what distance before the obstruction should you place the warning triangle?

a 25 metres (82 feet)

b 45 metres (147 feet)

c 100 metres (328 feet)

d 150 metres (492 feet)

Question 50

Mark one answer

Your motorcycle has broken down on a motorway. How will you know the direction of the nearest emergency telephone?

a By walking with the flow of traffic

b By following an arrow on a marker post

c By walking against the flow of traffic

d By remembering where the last phone was

Question 51

Mark one answer

You have broken down on a two-way road. You have a warning triangle.
It should be displayed

a on the roof of your vehicle

b at least 150 metres (492 feet) behind your vehicle

c at least 45 metres (147 feet) behind your vehicle

d just behind your vehicle

Q.Question 52

Mark three answers

The police may ask you to produce which three of these documents following an accident?

a Vehicle registration document

b Driving licence

c Theory test certificate

d Insurance certificate

e MOT test certificate

f Road tax disc

Question 53

Mark four answers

You are involved in an accident with another vehicle. Someone is injured. Your vehicle is damaged. Which FOUR of the following should you find out?

a Whether the driver owns the other vehicle involved

b The other driver's name, address and telephone number

c The make and registration number of the other vehicle

d The occupation of the other driver

e The details of the other driver's vehicle insurance

f Whether the other driver is licensed to drive

Question 54

Mark one answer

You should use the engine cut-out switch to

a stop the engine in an emergency
b stop the engine on short journeys
c save wear on the ignition switch
d start the engine if you lose the key

Question 55

Mark one answer

At a railway level crossing the red light signal continues to flash after a train has gone by. What should you do?

a Phone the signal operator
b Alert drivers behind you
c Wait
d Proceed with caution

Question 56

Mark three answers

You break down on a level crossing. The lights have not yet begun to flash. Which THREE things should you do?

a Telephone the signal operator
b Leave your vehicle and get everyone clear
c Walk down the track and signal the next train
d Move the vehicle if a signal operator tells you to
e Tell drivers behind what has happened

Question 57

Mark one answer

You have stalled in the middle of a level crossing and cannot restart the engine. The warning bell starts to ring. You should

a get out and clear of the crossing
b run down the track to warn the signal operator
c carry on trying to restart the engine
d push the vehicle clear of the crossing

Question 58

Mark one answer

You are travelling on a motorway. A bag falls from your motorcycle. There are valuables in the bag. What should you do?

a Go back carefully and collect the bag as quickly as possible
b Stop wherever you are and pick up the bag, but only when there is a safe gap
c Stop on the hard shoulder and use the emergency telephone to inform the police
d Stop on the hard shoulder and then retrieve the bag yourself

Question 59

Mark <u>one</u> answer

Your vehicle has broken down on an automatic railway level crossing. What should you do FIRST?

a Get everyone out of the vehicle and clear of the crossing

b Phone the signal operator so that trains can be stopped

c Walk along the track to give warning to any approaching trains

d Try to push the vehicle clear of the crossing as soon as possible

Question 60

Mark <u>two</u> answers

Your tyre bursts while you are driving. Which TWO things should you do?

a Pull on the handbrake

b Brake as quickly as possible

c Pull up slowly at the side of the road

d Hold the steering wheel firmly to keep control

e Continue on at a normal speed

Question 61

Mark <u>two</u> answers

Which TWO things should you do when a front tyre bursts?

a Apply the handbrake to stop the vehicle

b Brake firmly and quickly

c Let the vehicle roll to a stop

d Hold the steering wheel lightly

e Grip the steering wheel firmly

Question 62

Mark <u>one</u> answer

Your vehicle has a puncture on a motorway. What should you do?

a Drive slowly to the next service area to get assistance

b Pull up on the hard shoulder. Change the wheel as quickly as possible

c Pull up on the hard shoulder. Use the emergency phone to get assistance

d Switch on your hazard lights. Stop in your lane

Question 63

Mark <u>one</u> answer

You see a car on the hard shoulder of a motorway with a HELP pennant displayed. This means the driver is most likely to be

a a disabled person

b first aid trained

c a foreign visitor

d a rescue patrol person

Question 64

Mark <u>one</u> answer

On the motorway the hard shoulder should be used

a to answer a mobile phone

b when an emergency arises

c for a short rest when tired

d to check a road atlas

Question 65

Mark two answers

What TWO safeguards could you take against fire risk to your vehicle?

- Keep water levels above maximum
- Carry a fire extinguisher
- Avoid driving with a full tank of petrol
- Use unleaded petrol
- Check out any strong smell of petrol
- Use low octane fuel

Answers and explanations

Q001 a
Q002 b
Q003 a
Q004 a
Q005 b, e
Q006 a, b
Q007 a
Q008 a, d, e
Q009 a, b, c, e
Q010 d, e, f
Q011 a, d, e
Q012 a
Q013 b
Q014 b, c, d, e
Q015 d
Q016 b Warning other traffic first helps stop the accident getting even worse.
Q017 a, b, e
Q018 a

Q019 a, c, f
Injuries should be dealt with in the order Airway, Breathing then Circulation and bleeding.
Q020 a
Q021 a, b, d
Q022 a, c, e
Note that these are the things to which you should give urgent priority.
Q023 d, e, f
Q024 a, b, e
You should not move injured people unless they are in danger; nor should you give them anything to drink.
Q025 a, c, f
Q026 a, e
Q027 a, c, d, e
Q028 c
Q029 b, c
Q030 c, d, e
Q031 a
Q032 b Note that this is the FIRST thing to do. By warning other traffic you help reduce the risk of more collisions.
Q033 b
Q034 b, d, e
Q035 b
Q036 c
Q037 d
Q038 b

Answers and explanations

Q039 c, d

Q040 d

Q041 c

Q042 c

Q043 b If you move the casualty you may worsen their injury.

Q044 d

Q045 b

Q046 d

Q047 b, c, d

Q048 c 45 metres is recommended on two-way roads and 150 metres on a dual carriageway. You should not use a warning triangle on a motorway; it is too dangerous.

Q049 b

Q050 b

Q051 c

Q052 b, d, e

Q053 a, b, c, e

Q054 a The engine cut-out switch stops the engine and shuts off all electrical circuits, thus reducing the risk of fire in an accident.

Q055 c This usually means another train is coming.

Q056 a, b, d

Q057 a A train may arrive within seconds so 'a' is the only safe possibility.

Q058 c It would be extremely dangerous to try and retrieve the bag yourself.

Q059 a Your first action is to get everyone to safety.

Q060 c, d You will need both hands firmly on the wheel in order to control the car, and using the gears or brakes is likely to make your car swerve. When possible, it is safest just to let your car roll to a halt at the side of the road.

Q061 c, e

Q062 c The hard shoulder of a motorway is a dangerous place and 'c' is the safest course of action. It can be particularly dangerous to try to change an offside wheel as you may be very close to fast-moving traffic in the left-hand lane.

Q063 a

Q064 b

Q065 b, e

Theory Test Questions

2001/2002

Vehicle Loading

Question 1

Mark one answer

Are passengers allowed to ride in a caravan that is being towed?

a Yes, if they are over fourteen

b No, not at any time

c Only if all the seats in the towing vehicle are full

d Only if a stabilizer is fitted

Question 2

Mark one answer

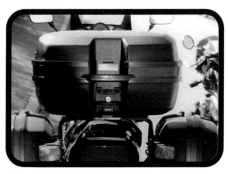

Carrying a heavy load in your top box may

a cause high speed weave

b cause a puncture

c use less fuel

d improve stability

Question 3

Mark one answer

You are towing a caravan along a motorway. The caravan begins to swerve from side to side. What should you do?

a Ease off the accelerator slowly

b Steer sharply from side to side

c Do an emergency stop

d Speed up very quickly

Question 4

Mark one answer

Heavy loads in a motorcycle top box may

a improve stability

b cause low-speed wobble

c cause a puncture

d improve braking

Question 5

Mark one answer

Who is responsible for making sure that a vehicle is not overloaded?

a The driver of the vehicle
b The owner of the items being carried
c The person who loaded the vehicle
d The licensing authority

Question 6

Mark one answer

A trailer on a motorcycle must be no wider than

a 1 metre (3 feet 3 inches)
b 0.5 metre (1 foot 8 inches)
c 1.5 metres (4 feet 11 inches)
d 2 metres (6 feet 6 inches)

Question 7

Mark two answers

Overloading your vehicle can seriously affect the

a gearbox
b steering
c handling
d battery life
e journey time

Question 8

Mark two answers

To carry a pillion passenger your motorcycle should be fitted with

a rear footrests
b an engine of 250cc or over
c a top box
d a grab handle
e a proper passenger seat

Question 9

Mark two answers

On which TWO occasions might you inflate your tyres to more than the recommended normal pressure?

a When the roads are slippery
b When driving fast for a long distance
c When the tyre tread is worn below 2mm
d When carrying a heavy load
e When the weather is cold
f When the vehicle is fitted with anti-lock brakes

Question 10

Mark one answer

Who is responsible for making sure that a motorcycle is not overloaded?

a The rider of the motorcycle
b The owner of the items being carried
c The licensing authority
d The owner of the motorcycle

Question 11

Mark one answer

Any load carried on a roof rack MUST be

a securely fastened when driving

b carried only when strictly necessary

c as light as possible

d covered with plastic sheeting

Question 12

Mark one answer

Before fitting a sidecar to a motorcycle you should

a have the wheels balanced

b have the engine tuned

c pass the extended bike test

d check that the motorcycle is suitable

Question 13

Mark one answer

A heavy load on your roof rack will

a improve the road holding

b reduce the stopping distance

c make the steering lighter

d reduce stability

Question 14

Mark two answers

Overloading your motorcycle can seriously affect the

a gearbox

b steering

c handling

d battery life

e journey time

Question 15

Mark three answers

Which THREE are suitable restraints for a child under three years?

a A child seat

b An adult holding a child

c An adult seat belt

d A lap belt

e A harness

f A baby carrier

Question 16

Mark one answer

Any load that is carried on a luggage rack MUST be

a securely fastened when riding

b carried only when strictly necessary

c visible when you are riding

d covered with plastic sheeting

Question 17

Mark one answer

Your vehicle is fitted with child safety door locks. You should use these so that children inside the car cannot open

a the right-hand doors

b the left-hand doors

c the rear doors

d any of the doors

Question 18

Mark one answer

You want to tow a trailer with your motorcycle. Which one applies?

a The motorcycle should be attached to a sidecar

b The trailer should weigh more than the motorcycle

c The trailer should be fitted with brakes

d The trailer should not be more than 1 metre (3 feet 3 inches) wide

Question 19

Mark one answer

You are planning to tow a caravan. Which of these will mostly help to aid the vehicle handling?

a A jockey-wheel fitted to the towbar

b Power steering fitted to the towing vehicle

c Anti-lock brakes fitted to the towing vehicle

d A stabiliser fitted to the towbar

Question 20

Mark one answer

If a trailer swerves or snakes when you are towing it you should

a ease off the throttle and reduce your speed

b let go of the handlebars and let it correct itself

c brake hard and hold the brake on

d increase your speed as quickly as possible

Question 21

Mark one answer

A trailer must stay securely hitched-up to the towing vehicle. What additional safety device can be fitted to the trailer braking system?

a Stabiliser

b Jockey wheel

c Corner steadies

d Breakaway cable

Question 22

Mark one answer

If a trailer swerves or snakes when you are towing it you should

a ease off the accelerator and reduce your speed

b let go of the steering wheel and let it correct itself

c brake hard and hold the pedal down

d increase your speed as quickly as possible

Question 23

Mark <u>one</u> answer

You have a side-car fitted to your motorcycle. What effect will it have?

a Reduce stability

b Make steering lighter

c Increase stopping distance

d Increase fuel economy

Question 24

Mark <u>one</u> answer

How can you stop a caravan snaking from side to side?

a Turn the steering wheel slowly to each side

b Accelerate to increase your speed

c Stop as quickly as you can

d Slow down very gradually

Question 25

Mark <u>two</u> answers

When riding with a sidecar attached for the first time you should

a keep your speed down

b be able to stop more quickly

c accelerate quickly round bends

d approach corners more carefully

Question 26

Mark <u>two</u> answers

You are towing a small trailer on a busy three-lane motorway. All the lanes are open. You must

a not exceed 60 mph

b not overtake

c have a stabiliser fitted

d use only the left and centre lanes

Question 27

Mark <u>two</u> answers

You want to tow a trailer behind your motorcycle. You should

a display a 'long vehicle' sign

b fit a larger battery

c have a full motorcycle licence

d ensure that your engine is more than 125cc

e ensure that your motorcycle has shaft drive

Question 28

Mark <u>one</u> answer

When may a learner motorcyclist carry a pillion passenger?

a If the passenger holds a full licence

b Not at any time

c If the rider is undergoing training

d If the passenger is over 21

Question 29

Mark three answers

Which THREE must a learner motorcyclist under 21 NOT do?

a Ride a motorcycle with an engine capacity greater than 125cc

b Pull a trailer

c Carry a pillion passenger

d Ride faster than 30 mph

e Use the right-hand lane on dual carriageways

Question 30

Mark one answer

Pillion passengers should

a have a provisional motorcycle licence

b be lighter than the rider

c always wear a helmet

d signal for the rider

Question 31

Mark one answer

Pillion passengers should

a give the rider directions

b lean with the rider when going round bends

c check the road behind for the rider

d give arm signals for the rider

Question 32

Mark three answers

When carrying extra weight on a motorcycle, you may need to make adjustments to the

a headlight

b gears

c suspension

d tyres

e footrests

Question 33

Mark one answer

To obtain the full category 'A' licence through the accelerated or direct access scheme, your motorcycle must be

a solo with maximum power 25 kw (33 bhp)

b solo with maximum power of 11 kw (14.6 bhp)

c fitted with a sidecar and have minimum power of 35 kw (46.6 bhp)

d solo with minimum power of 35 kw (46.6 bhp)

Question 34

Mark one answer

When you are going around a corner your pillion passenger should

a give arm signals for you

b check behind for other vehicles

c lean with you on bends

d lean to one side to see ahead

Question 35

Mark <u>one</u> <u>answer</u>

Which of these may need to be adjusted when carrying a pillion passenger?

a Indicators

b Exhaust

c Fairing

d Headlight

Question 36

Mark <u>three</u> <u>answers</u>

Your motorcycle is fitted with a top box. It is unwise to carry a heavy load in the top box because it may

a reduce stability

b improve stability

c make turning easier

d cause high-speed weave

e cause low-speed wobble

f increase fuel economy

Question 37

Mark <u>one</u> <u>answer</u>

You are towing a trailer with your motorcycle. You should remember that your

a stopping distance may increase

b fuel consumption will improve

c tyre grip will increase

d stability will improve

Answers and explanations

Q001   b

Q002   a

Q003   a

Q004   b

Q005   a

Q006   a

Q007   b, c

Q008   a, e

Q009   b, d

Q010   a

Q011   a The word 'MUST' in the question makes 'a' correct.

Q012   d

Q013   d A heavy load on the roof will shift the centre of gravity of your vehicle and could make you more likely to skid or roll over.

Q014   b, c

Q015   a, e, f

Q016   a

Q017   c

Q018   d The laden weight of the trailer must not exceed 150kg or two-thirds of the kerbside weight of the motorcycle, whichever is less.

Q019   d

Q020   a

Q021   d

Answers and explanations

Q022 a Options 'b', 'c' or 'd' would all be likely to make the problem worse.

Q023 c The side-car is extra weight and is likely to increase your overall stopping distance.

Q024 d

Q025 a, d

You will need to adapt your riding technique when riding a bike with a side-car, particularly on bends and when turning. The side-car must be steered because you cannot lean the machine over.

Q026 a, d

Q027 c, d

Q028 b

Q029 a, b, c

Q030 c

Q031 b

Q032 a, c, d

Q033 d

Q034 c

Q035 d

Q036 a, d, e

Q037 a

Notes

For information on learning to drive or ride with a BSM instructor please contact your local BSM centre on:

08457 276 276

BSM instructors operate under a franchise with
The British School of Motoring Limited, the largest organisation of its kind
in the world.

The three additional books in the series, *Pass Your Driving Test*, *Pass Your Driving Theory Test* and *Practice Sessions* are available from all BSM centres and from all good bookshops.